Institutional Change
from Within

Changing the Light Bulb Series

Series Editor: David Silverberg

The intention of the series is to explore and illustrate case studies of, and learning from, the iconic question of "how many _____'s does it take to change the light bulb?" The first two books in the series center around how this question applies to the field of higher education, with one text highlighting issues of Leadership & Identity (Empowerment at the Tower: Leadership and Identity in Higher Education) and the other book focusing on issues of Teaching & Learning (Institutional Change from Within: Teaching and Learning in Higher Education). There are 21 chapter authors/co-authors in all from 11 institutions in 10 states. The books feature their reporting on how transformation initiatives occurred at their college/university, what challenges arose, and how they overcame those challenges. Interviews with the authors are included as well as probing questions for the reader.

Institutional Change from Within

Teaching and Learning in Higher Education

Edited by David Silverberg

ROWMAN & LITTLEFIELD
Lanham • Boulder • New York • London

Published by Rowman & Littlefield
A wholly owned subsidiary of The Rowman & Littlefield Publishing Group, Inc.
4501 Forbes Boulevard, Suite 200, Lanham, Maryland 20706
www.rowman.com

Unit A, Whitacre Mews, 26–34 Stannary Street, London SE11 4AB

British Library Cataloguing in Publication Information Available

Library of Congress Cataloging-in-Publication Data Available

ISBN 978-1-4758-3597-7 (cloth : alk. paper)
ISBN 978-1-4758-3598-4 (pbk. : alk. paper)
ISBN 978-1-4758-3599-1 (electronic)

∞™ The paper used in this publication meets the minimum requirements of American
National Standard for Information Sciences—Permanence of Paper for Printed Library
Materials, ANSI/NISO Z39.48–1992.

Printed in the United States of America

Dedicated to Steph, Tessa, Cal, Dan, mom, and dad.

Contents

Acknowledgments

I'd like to thank my wife, Stephanie, for her amazing support of my inspirations and our two children, Cal and Tessa, for inspiring me to be the best dad I can be. I'd also like to thank Dr. Gene Linton (dean of the Founders School of Continuing Education, executive director of Professional Development, Ashland University) and Dr. Todd Marshall (associate provost, College of Online and Adult Studies, Ashland University) for their dynamic leadership and ongoing support. A special thank you goes to Lynn Meister (technical editor), Alan Buttar (Muse Graphic Design), and Dr. Tom Koerner (vice president and publisher for Education Issues, Rowman & Littlefield) for their patience and expertise.

Introduction

With so much change going on in the world today, technologically, politically, environmentally—you name it—I started to wonder: what, and how, change is occurring in one of the most traditional and at times calcified industries: higher education.

So I collected stories from eleven institutions in ten states—twenty-one academics in all—and compiled those as edited chapters with follow-up interviews and questions for the reader. What started out as one volume expanded into two sister texts, one focusing on teaching and learning and the other highlighting leadership and identity.

The burning question I asked myself and the chapter authors was, "How many academics does it take to change the light bulb in higher education?" This innocent question got far more spontaneous laughter, and varied response, than I could have imagined. I heard everything from "zero" to a comment about it being an elastic number based on the scope of the change initiative. Those responses are included in these texts along the institutional case studies written by authors from the respective college/university and their answers to my probing questions.

One surprise to me, and to many of the authors, was the inherent joy and insight that came from the reflection involved in writing their institution's transformation story. I have included their moving insights at the beginning of each chapter to provide some insight into their respective learning journey through this process. My hope is that their words inspire readers to consider ways of intentionally reflecting on their own initiatives as a way of deepening their experience and improving the transformational process.

Each chapter includes some background about the change initiative, information about their successes and challenges, insights about the change initiative, and a few key lessons learned. Interview questions and answers highlight the author's insights about the number of academics needed to change the light bulb, personal reflections about how they became agents of change, and advice for others who want to create change at their own institution of higher learning.

This volume on teaching and learning features chapters written by authors from Roosevelt University, Illinois; SUNY, the College at Brockport, New York; American College of Education, Indiana; University of Pittsburgh, Pennsylvania; and University of Arkansas, Arkansas. I hope that these chapters and the transparent insights of their authors help lay the foundation for growth and innovation within you and for your institution.

Light Bulb Motif

The question of "How many academics does it take to change light bulb?" offers a fun and insightful framework for exploring the way things work or don't work while also unveiling possible levers for meaningful change. To help operationalize this idea, I'd like to suggest this conceptual representation of a light bulb that I hope will support your professional growth and that of your college or university. In this image the filament, wires, and stem are replaced by the lower-case Greek letter delta, which is often used to represent a state of change in science, mathematics, and other fields. This honors the kind of *change from within* that so many chapter authors describe as a surprise benefit of reflecting on their journey as change agents.

Figure 0FM.1. Light.bulb.motif.artwork

The "Light Bulb Moment Worksheet" (appendix) was designed with this motif in mind to stimulate personal reflection and effective implementation. I invite you to use this worksheet to generate light bulb moments at your college or university.

Chapter 1

Improving Instruction When Transitioning to Online Service Models: Opportunities, Challenges, and Complexities

Brad Cawn

Roosevelt University, Illinois

How many academics does it take to change a light bulb?

0

In this chapter an adjunct professor of language and literature, Brad Cawn writes about how instruction improved as part of Roosevelt University's transition to online instructional models. I was moved to hear Brad's thoughts about the reflective benefits of writing the chapter:

> *I can't express enough to you that I really actually did enjoy writing [this piece], it was kind of like a capstone in a way. Not just simply reflecting on "this is what I did," it was more like "how does it dovetail with a lot of larger things that are happening? What am I learning? What is the field learning? Where do we go with this knowledge?" And I feel like that synthesis was abuzz of writing.*

INTRODUCTION

The twenty-first century has not been kind to university-based teacher education. Though the field saw many innovations in the kinds and delivery of its service models, it has been the subject of repeated critiques, as both outside organizations (Levine, 2006; National Council on Teacher Quality, 2013) and a former secretary of the U.S. Department of Education himself (Duncan, 2009) bemoaned the "persistent mediocrity" of teacher preparation programs.

Though an unprecedented amount of public and private monies have flowed into teacher preparation during the years of the Obama presidency (Wilson, 2014), much of the resources that came with it were dedicated to accountability policies and measures, with the goal of making teacher education programs "prove it" when it came to the impact teacher candidates had on students; most cannot. Meanwhile, the private sector has begun to see teacher education as a space "ripe for disruption" (Liu, 2013; Zeichner & Pena-Sandoval, 2015).

But economic forces have been equally as disruptive. Demand for teachers, particularly those prepared and able to support diverse learners, has increased over the last decade; the supply of new teachers, however, has not, with enrollments in teacher preparation programs down, on average, by 35 percent—in some cases much higher (Sutcher, Darling-Hammond, & Carver-Thomas, 2016). The negative perception of schools and the profession of teaching, persistent fears about the instability of employment in the profession, and the changing values and career interests of young professionals—all have contributed to a declining interest in the profession that cannot be easily rectified through increased marketing by programs or pay increases by K–12 schools. Further compounding matters, increased competition from alternative certification programs (Teach for America) and online-only programs (e.g., University of Phoenix), which often provide cheaper and/or faster certification, chipped away at the veritable monopoly the 1,500 or so university-based teacher preparation programs held over the teacher induction business.

BACKGROUND AND CHALLENGES

Faced with a dwindling market and increased competition, university-based teacher preparation programs, long thought to be the "cash cows" of professional preparation programs (Labaree, 2008), have faced a two-pronged challenge: (1) reducing or restricting costs while (2) turning, often for the first time, to try to market to new or wider audiences. Over the last decade, an increasingly viable option to achieve both needs has been to adapt or expand programming models to an online environment, thereby reducing the costs per credit hour of certification and increasing the number of potential applications. The tactic is not without its challenges, however, most notably the risk of a price war, with area or regional institutions competing for a limited application pool by undercutting one another on credit hour costs.

All of this has transpired at the same time as the field has begun to coalesce around a vision of teacher preparation that mirrored the rigorous training and induction methods of high-status professions, including those of medicine and law. It may seem peculiarly ironic that the field of teaching lacked clarity and consensus on teaching itself, but empirical evidence in support of so-called core pedagogies (McDonald, Kazemi, & Kavanagh, 2013) and groundswells of support for pedagogical reform are only very recent trends (see Grossman, Hammerness, & McDonald, 2009). Chief among these changes were calls for "clinically rich" preparation experiences (NCATE Blue Ribbon Panel Report, 2010), in which teacher candidates would not only get more time in school settings prior to becoming a teacher of record but more coaching and content on that field work; and a move to more "practice-based" methods, in which novice educators would receive hands-on training in a set of "high-leverage practices" (Ball & Forzani, 2009)—say, introducing or assigning an activity, or facilitating a discussion—that they could then replicate in their own classrooms from their very outset of their careers. Increasingly, leading voices in the field (e.g., Cochran-Smith, 2015; Deans for Impact, 2017) have advocated for scaling of such practices.

Thus, many teacher preparation programs encounter competing agendas on their way to program improvement: increase efficiency to ensure survival; improve services to ensure relevance. In this formative period of both significant economic pressure and pedagogical experimentation, method and medium often initially appear at odds with one another: moving to an asynchronous medium creates new challenges for implementing "practice-based" methods of teacher education; reducing the length or demands of certification can hamper the ability to engage in scaffolded, meaningful "clinically rich" learning experiences. But the tension also creates new opportunities; for it is here that the future of teacher education will be forged.

Tension and opportunity: these are the themes of the case study presented in this chapter. It's the story of one program working through the changes—with change itself becoming a tool for learning and continuous improvement. It's a story still in motion—in fact, the motion is the continuous telling and adapting of the story as the program responds to significant changes internally and externally.

Setting and Background

Roosevelt University is an urban public institution of roughly 7,000 students located in downtown Chicago; a satellite campus exists in a suburb to the northwest of the city. With a particular focus on preparation for the professions, and with one of the most diverse student populations in the country, the university's primary, if unstated, purpose is to provide skilled professionals, such as teachers and pharmacists, for the region's service economy. The College of Education's offerings follow suit: all of its degree programs lead to certification to practice the respective area in the state of Illinois. Most programs in the college have significant practicum components.

The graduate program in Reading is no exception, drawing mainly practicing teachers—already possessing undergraduate degrees in education—and centering its programming around role-specific endorsements: reading teacher or ESL/second language specialist. Lured by their school districts' subsidizing of graduate studies and/or tying pay increases to additional education, however, the program draws a significant number of new teachers, many of whom enter with goals less centered on pursuing a specific literacy role in their schools but on obtaining a graduate degree or increasing their salary.

Several other colleges of education in the Chicagoland area offer graduate degrees and/or endorsements in Reading, creating a relatively stable market for students for many years; however, the decline in teacher preparation enrollment following the Great Recession led to significant market disruption. When other area graduate programs moved online and reduced credit hour costs, Roosevelt experienced a significant reduction in enrollment, prompting its own move to an online-only program in the fall of 2015. Efforts to market the program—its flexibility, its affordability—were increased.

As a course designer and subsequent instructor in the shifting program, I was tasked with redesigning several of the courses in the program for online delivery; the institution retained the practicum component of the degree, a summer-only course in which students worked as tutors with striving readers. Initially, the mandate was simple: transition the previous program into an online environment, maintaining the core objectives of the courses and, where feasible and relevant, the content as well. There were neither the funds nor the focus for a new vision of how to implement teacher education.

Having taught teaching at a number of different institutions and settings—undergraduate and graduate, traditional and alternative—I knew the drill. As any instructor would in a similar scenario, I kept the bones of the coursework and updated content based on new and/or missing literature; I tweaked the main projects and assessments of the coursework to reflect what I felt were more "authentic" applications of the applicant. Knowing the importance of social activity and collaboration to learning, I added weekly group work in several courses, hoping to bridge the distance and asynchronous medium by connecting students through meaningful tasks.

Though the program administrators and myself were deeply versed in literacy and literacy education matters, none of us had experience designing online teacher education, and that inexperience was evident in the assumptions made. We assumed that maintaining or improving the course content or focus would ensure an efficient or effective shift in the service model; it didn't. We assumed that students would experience the course similarly to how they would when it was face-to-face; they didn't. And we assumed students would treat the coursework the same way they did when face-to-face; they *definitely* didn't.

The first months were, admittedly, rough. Without constant and significant contact, content repeatedly didn't "stick"; collaboration and flipped instruction did not make a major dent in the reality that many students simply did not have the experience and/or training with either the knowledge base underlying literacy acquisition and development or the highly complex work of enacting it in practice (e.g., diagnosing reading difficulties, leading staff development). Students, at various stages in the program and with varying demands in their professional lives outside of class, did not want to complete coursework online in discrete weekly chunks; rather, they wanted the freedom to engage the course as befit their schedules and interests. Perhaps because of previous experiences with online coursework that merely tasked them to post in message boards and/or take rudimentary quizzes, they balked at the rigor of the work and the amount of collaboration; tensions in groups arose almost immediately.

Change Initiative

Clearly, there was work to be done. But this time it had to be the right work: improvement focused not on medium or curriculum but the student learning experience. It seems almost self-evident to say, yet we forget it all too often: it all starts with *learning*—it's not just the end goal but also how we determine what's next. To make the programming more learning-centered, we had to focus on what we knew about their students: their work, their perceptions, their needs. In addition to formal course evaluations, I ran informal surveys with students on the coursework and proposed changes, consulted with a focal group of students directly about their experiences in the program, and looked at quite a bit of student work to understand where instruction failed and where misconceptions or partial understanding lay. Painful, but it very quickly revealed practical solutions.

The most practical and impactful of those solutions was also the least flashy and technical. Several students had trouble with the rigor and pace of my Literacy Acquisition and Development course and underperformed academically against their own expectations; reflection on the implementation challenges led me to offer them a chance to improve their grade in the course, with additional support. Working side-by-side with the students again revealed that the difference-making practice for us was not going to be technological in nature; it was going to be the sort of behaviors that bridged the divide created by the technology. For students, it wasn't just that feedback was helpful; it was actually *instructive*.

Feedback. Lots of it. Continuous feedback. Directed feedback. Timely feedback. When your focus is laser-like on student understanding, changes to programming or curriculum become elementary: you make clearer articulations about outcomes and benchmarks, identify opportunities in process to assess and support students toward those articulations, and plan a range of supports of diverse learners. In my own coursework, everything centered around core competencies: I tightened the connection between the program standards and content, embedding those standards into the rubrics used to assess students' work on course projects; built in weekly means for students to get feedback from both me and their peers; and made individual check-ins and conferences a regular component of the course. With clear conceptions of what students must know and be able to do at various points in a given course, I knew precisely when and how to provide support to each student.

Situating progress monitoring as the foundation of the coursework enabled me to make more radical and creative changes to the course structure and sequence, not less. First, I shifted the idea of where learning occurred and what that learning entailed: no longer bound to the university-based classroom or online, and with a majority of students already practicing professionals, we were free to locate it in our students' classrooms, where they were facilitating learning of their own. Teaching tasks, curriculum materials, student work—all became records of practice to study the theory and practice of reading. And we could use theory and practice to study teaching, with concepts from readings being tested out in students' classrooms, with subsequent discussions in individual reflections or group/class discussions.

Second, with the courses being rebuilt around authentic tasks tied to fully articulated steps and expectations, project-based learning became much more feasible. Student choice was increased—whether through choosing the task, the readings, the process, etc.—and multiple pathways were enabled so that students could move through course material based on schedules and readiness. The Literacy Acquisition and Development course noted earlier, for instance, became built around a course-length literature review or self-study project, reflecting the academic research material that comprised a good chunk of the readings; these readings, in turn, supported an understanding of not only the underlying theory of literacy learning but also how to research it. The relevance and engagement of the content was now evident in practice, not just on paper.

SUCCESSES AND OBSTACLES

The original course designs were, by design, meant to be one-size-fits-all; they fit no one. The initial outcomes could hardly be called surprising: those students with more experience—either with teaching and/or with academic learning—and/or those more intrinsically motivated did well; those who did not were largely lost. Attrition and failure rates increased.

Rebuilding around the student learning experience mitigated a significant number of learning challenges; moreover, it individualized learning, enabling instructors to differentiate supports depending on students' unique learning challenges or opportunities. Focus of student tasks was put on the "doing" of the work—the key practices of the discipline and its roles—and on helping students appropriate this knowledge and tools in their own classrooms; focus of instructor efforts was on supporting individual students to make these connections. As many students noted on subsequent course evaluations, the theoretical started becoming practical.

A good example of the shift and its resulting impact can be seen in the program's Literacy Assessment course. Previously, and in the first year of online implementation, the course had been constructed as a survey of different ways to assess students' fluency or comprehension of what they read, particularly those for struggling readers; although students would test these instruments out in their own classrooms, the primary purpose was to focus on the measurement tool, not learning from what students know or could do on said assessment. The revisions flipped this focus: the key conceptual understanding of the course became assessment, particularly formative assessment, as a way of improving teaching; the key teaching points became how to understand and integrate assessment into instruction. The core task of the course became creating a comprehensive assessment program for their classrooms: students had to plan, design, and assess an intentional sequence of assessments to monitor their students' progress; they then had to design a collaboration session for/with their school-based colleagues to discuss the findings and future applications of the assessments. Throughout the process, they received ongoing feedback from me on their plan, their assessments, and their analysis and reporting of the results.

Concentrating on teaching through feedback allowed us to get much better on feedback and, subsequently, at teaching online writ large. Conferences with students became structured, scaffolded learning events, with time built in to discuss readings or data, dialogue about written feedback or upcoming assignments, or provide targeted instruction in an area of need (a misconception about a reading, say); as we got better at anticipating and responding to student needs, we began to differentiate tasks based on student understanding and readiness demonstrated during the conference. The quality of work, both in their enactment and written work, improved; we began to see excellence more equitably distributed. Students who underperformed in the first or second semester significantly improved the quality of the work in the improved course designs.

We should be careful not to underestimate the considerable shift in attitude and approach required of both teacher and student in order to make a learner-centered environment work—especially a virtual one. Faculty must switch their priorities and behavior from transmitting knowledge or skill to supporting its uptake in complex settings—no easy task in colleges of education, where many teacher educators are adjuncts and have little experience teaching this way. It requires a significant shift in how faculty utilize their time—not necessarily more of it, but more emphasis on student learning during learning. That means learning can't be reduced to chunks based on topic and/or timing; rather, it has to arise from and attend to the specific learning opportunities presented or needed by students as they are engaging in tasks.

Students, too, have to make significant shifts in their approach to schooling. Coursework cannot be seen as a discrete set of work to be accomplished in a single sitting; rather, as the work mirrors what they are learning through their practice, it has to be processed and built on consistently, in smaller and repeated activities and reflections. This is no easy task for students with day jobs, many of whom are in their first years in the professions; it also is contrary to the structure of schooling they received for decades prior to graduate study. When you couple that with students' assumptions and low expectations for online coursework, it shouldn't surprise that initially many expressed frustration with the demands of the coursework, and had difficulties adjusting to a learning environment where the core tasks continually required reflection, revision, and expansion. It takes time—and direct support—to adjust; some did not at first. Significant buy-in is needed: students need to know that the feedback they receive is not evaluative; rather, it leads to not only improved work but also deeper learning. Emphasis on the relational component of teaching becomes critical to such a goal, and the asynchronous nature of online, even with the addition of video conferencing, often impedes collaboration and trust.

LESSONS LEARNED

The Medium Is the Message—but Not All of It

Teaching online requires adapting methods to attend to the opportunities and constraints of asynchronous virtual environment, as well as to the different ways students interact with content. As we learned, an articulated program sequence and standards are not alone sufficient to ensure seamless transition to a different service model; attention must be given to the student learning experience in the specific context. The medium, not just the message, matters.

But teaching online *effectively* requires more than just the use of different methods; it requires a change in mindset about the purpose of instruction and the role of instructor in achieving it. Our progress came about not simply because of a shift in how we facilitated instruction in an online space but because our conception of instruction itself shifted toward meeting individual needs, situating learning inside of students' classroom practice, and reframing the instructor role as more coach/consultant than gatekeeper—it was only together that these elements improved both teaching and learning. We will continue to tweak our methods and calibrate content and expected outcomes, of course, but the real work of the program now occurs in the student interaction with relevant tasks in meaningful contexts, not a Learning Management System platform.

Program innovation, then, does not start with the service delivery model or instructional method; it likely doesn't end there, either. Rather, it centers on a radical redefinition of what it means to be a learner in a given field or profession and/or what it means to be a future practitioner; everything else supports it. We got better when student learning became the driver of implementation; our innovations—the use of the medium, the methods—did, too.

Change Is Easy; Sustaining It Is Hard

Lasting change may be difficult, but switches, reforms, and shifts are actually quite easy when external pressures—economic, political, etc.—necessitate them. The transition to an online-only graduate program described in this chapter was planned and implemented over the course of a single semester and summer; the enrollment numbers nearly tripled from the last year of the face-to-face program to the online program.

Retrospectively speaking, that was the easy part.

What's less easy is maintaining the change. Personnel will change; commitment to continuous improvement—whether from administrators, faculty, students, etc.—will wane. Can the program improvements be sustained if interest in teaching—or advanced teacher certification—continues to stagnate or decline? Or, if students continue to be surprised, if not occasionally resistant, by a more rigorous program model than what they might have expected from an online-only degree? Still to be determined. And it remains to be seen how financial challenges facing the university will affect the program long term—already it has forced the shuffling of course assignments, and it's still unclear how that has affected and will affect student learning.

The bulwark is the wisdom gleaned. In many ways, we were a "lean start-up": we launched with a minimal viable product and continued to make adjustments as we implemented. Development was agile, in large part because the number of hands-on deck remained small: those of us who designed the courses taught the courses, giving us both the space and agency to make improvements, especially on the fly. Ownership and expertise over both process and product ensured fidelity of implementation; close contact with students ensured consistent, meaningful feedback. There is something to be said here for starting small, whether by piloting with a small(er) cohort or gradually rolling out program components, and growing through learning first.

And there is something to be said for having a clear and shared purpose. Administrators, instructors, students—everyone needs to know the "WHY" of what is being done, not just the what or how. When purpose leads, method and content readily follow. We are not there yet as a program—and in teacher education, where adjuncts predominate, we might never be—but the clearer our articulations are about the rationale for our work and the way we work, the more it seems student learning sticks. If we remain consistent in our messaging across channels, buy-in is inevitable.

CONCLUSION

Teacher education is in many ways a "canary in the coal mine" of higher education: a kind of omen about how rapidly changing technological, market, and cultural forces might quickly and significantly shape academic programs and traditions long thought to be safe, reliable, implacable. The case study in this chapter suggests that the hyperfocus many institutions are putting on "innovation"—such as changing programming designs or program delivery models to reflect twenty-first-century possibilities and demands—is only part of a coherent response to such disruption; the other half is *being* innovative— that is, getting better organizationally at leading and managing change. Small data over Big Data, you might call it: a commitment to adopting learning stances and becoming a learning organization, to inquiry and reflection about the process and product of our efforts, to improving engagement with the students and stakeholders we serve. Committing to excellence even in—or because of!—challenging times: it could be the most innovative idea yet.

Interviews

"Light bulb moments" are often seen as being serendipitous and fleeting. I hope that the following interview questions and answers deepen understanding about how these moments can be cultivated and sustained. The "Light Bulb Moment Worksheet" (appendix) offers a framework for stimulating transformation at your college or university.

Changing the Light Bulb

David: How many academics does it take to change a light bulb?

Brad: Honestly, I would say zero and I'm going to say that because my sense is that if we're going to change the light bulb I don't know if we should self-identify as academics. I wonder if that term and real innovation are in conflict with one another. I think part of the way you change the light bulb is by repositioning your role, or the way in which you position yourself, or how you [self] identify and I think—particularly in my field—I think far too many people have identified with academics and proposed solutions only to see a lot of those ideas fail to be diffused or disseminated across systems . . . even within their own institutions. So I wonder if repositioning or renaming ourselves is actually part of it and has nothing to do with "academic" or at the academy at all.

I hope my story reflects that in a lot of ways a disruption is kind of necessary in roles as well as the actual delivery method of service models and whatnot. I really feel like it's time for some serious navel gazing and some action from institutions; some really hard reflections about our roles and commitment to the things that we say we're committed to it in our missions or visions.

Question for Reader Reflection

In what ways would reframing the role of academicians help to advance change at your institution?

Change Agency

David: How has your life prepared you to be a change agent?

Brad: I've seen how bureaucracies work and don't work and I've been a learner throughout all of the environments: [I've been] a high school teacher; I've worked in the central office of a large urban district; I have worked for organizations on research projects; I've taught in higher education now for going on seven years this fall. I've been in a lot of systems and, you know, many of them are not set up to be learning organizations or learning systems. And so I've taken on that brunt myself in a lot of ways and a lot of that has to do with "failing better"—I believe the term is often used—or "failing up."

Question for Reader Reflection

What have you learned from previous professional challenges that could help you generate change at your current institution?

Advice

David: What advice do you have for others who want to transform higher education?

Brad: I would say . . . in the broadest philosophical sense, I would really focus on listening. I feel like we all know this, like in our minds we know this, but I think we get siloed too easily or too excited about innovating and making substantive change. We form committees, we have these really good design ideas, we sit and we read the research, or we see case studies of other institutions, and we get really excited about it. And I think what we have to remember is that innovation, like anything else, is completely situative, right? It's entirely based on the particular context, stakeholders, systems that are in place in any given institution. And I think part of it when doing that initial analysis is taking account of things (the unique qualities of the institution which are the benefits, the great strengths), but not necessarily assuming that because a program, model, or an innovation is exciting means that it will be successful in your institution. So this idea is an opportunity to listen, to get a wide variety of input. I think that is really key.

Question for Reader Reflection

How could listening more attentively improve your ability to generate transformation at your college or university?

REFERENCES

Ball, D. L., & Forzani, F. M. (2009). The work of teaching and the challenge for teacher education. *Journal of Teacher Education, 60*(5), 497–511.

Cochran-Smith, M. (2015). Keeping teaching complex: Policy, research and practice. *Venue, 4*, 1–11.

Deans for Impact. (2017). *Practice with purpose: The emerging science of teacher expertise*. Austin, TX: Author.

Duncan, A. (2009, October). Teacher preparation: Reforming the uncertain profession. Remarks of Secretary Arne Duncan at Teachers College, Columbia University. Retrieved from http://www2.ed.gov/news/speeches/2009/10/10222009.html

Grossman, P., Hammerness, K., & McDonald, M. (2009). Redefining teaching, reimagining teacher education. *Teachers and Teaching: Theory and Practice, 15*(2), 273–289.

Labaree, D. F. (2008). An uneasy relationship: The history of teacher education in the university. In M. Cochran-Smith, S. Feiman-Nemser, & J. McIntyre (Eds.), *Handbook of research on teacher education* (3rd ed., pp. 290–306). New York, NY: Routledge.

Levine, A. (2006). Educating school teachers. Education Schools Project.

Liu, M. (2013). Disrupting teacher education. *Education Next, 13*(3). Retrieved January 10, 2014 from http://educationnext.org/disrupting-teacher-education/

McDonald, M., Kazemi, E., & Kavanagh, S. S. (2013). Core practices and pedagogies of teacher education: A call for a common language and collective activity. *Journal of Teacher Education, 64*(5), 378–386.

National Council on Teacher Quality. (2013, June). *Teacher prep review: A review of the nation's teacher prep programs*. Washington, DC: Author.

NCATE Blue Ribbon Panel Report. (2010). Transforming teacher education through clinical practice: A national strategy to prepare effective teachers. National Council on Accreditation of Teacher Education.

Sutcher, L., Darling-Hammond, L., & Carver-Thomas, D. (2016). A coming crisis in teaching? *Teacher Supply, Demand, and Shortages in the US*. Learning Policy Institute. Washington, DC.

Wilson, S. M. (2014). Innovation and the evolving system of US teacher preparation. *Theory into Practice, 53*(3), 183–195.

Zeichner, K., & Pena-Sandoval, C. (2015). Venture philanthropy and teacher education policy in the US: The role of the New Schools Venture Fund. *Teachers College Record, 117*(6), 1–44.

Chapter 2

Preparing Metacognitive Educational Leaders

Heather Donnelly and Dr. Jeff Linn

SUNY, The College at Brockport, New York

How many academics does it take to change a light bulb?

1 or 2

In this chapter Heather Donnelly, visiting assistant professor, and Dr. Jeff Linn, department chair, write about their efforts to develop metacognitive educational leaders at SUNY, The College of Brockport. At the end of my interview, Jeff shared how much the reflection involved in writing the chapter matched the message of their work:

> *If anything is at the heart of our chapter it's the idea of metacognition. The idea of reflection, of metacognition, is central to our program. And so to be able to do that [very process here] really helps to crystallize my thinking. Writing this chapter was a gift.*

I was so pleased to hear Heather's comments about the benefits of the reflective process:

> *It was really a great experience for [us] to sit down to write this because we reflected so much on the work that he's done so far in the department, that we've done together, where we are, and where we still need to go. The process of writing this for us was a time to celebrate, a time to collaborate, and a time to set some more goals for where we want to go in this upcoming school year. Like we just talked yesterday about [how] "we've got to get together this summer . . . and do this, this, and this." And so I think that speaks to the process of writing the chapter.*

INTRODUCTION

Leadership is, at its essence, "the capacity to generate energy and passion in others through action."[1]

There are higher expectations placed on educational leaders today than ever before. They are expected to build and maintain relationships with all stakeholders while simultaneously making decisions that impact all of these stakeholder groups. They are required to solve problems, manage time, and collaborate, while also independently resolving time-sensitive issues on a daily basis. Educational leaders must have extensive knowledge of effective instruction, social-emotional learning, and trauma-informed and culturally responsive practices. In addition, most educational leaders work an average of sixty to seventy hours per week, yet are told to be sure to "take care of yourself" to avoid burnout while continuing to engage in their own professional learning to remain on top of current educational trends and legislative changes.

While balancing all of the above expectations, more than anything, educational leaders are expected to *move* people.

As professors of Educational Administration at The College at Brockport, a local branch of State University of New York (SUNY) just outside of Rochester, NY, we are obligated to not only understand the shifting landscape in education and its direct impact on educational leaders, but also have a commitment to prepare future leaders to be successful in this changing climate. In addition to the above list of expectations, our American school system has experienced drastic changes in just the last ten years—changes that occurred so quickly yet educational leadership has not kept up. Countries such as Finland, Canada, Japan, and New Zealand—while not facing all of the same challenges as U.S. schools—professionalize education and value educators, and provide models of quality leadership for our educational systems. Yet our schools present an image of teachers and leaders walking through quicksand, unable to move forward while being devoured by the fast-paced changing demands placed upon them.

THE SHIFTING LANDSCAPE OF AMERICAN EDUCATION

So how has education changed? Let's examine the list below by thinking about the direct impact these changes have on our role as professors of Educational Leadership.

- Increasing gender diversity in school leadership: Traditionally, school leaders have been males, but in the last two decades we have seen a shift in the percentage of women stepping into leadership roles in schools. According to a study conducted by the National Center for Educational Statistics (NCES) within the U.S. Department of Education (USDOE),[2] the percentage of female principals increased in public schools between 1987–1988 and 2011–2012 from 25 to 52 percent. Specifically, during the 2011–2012 school year, 54 percent of new public school principals were women.[3] Enrollment statistics in our own program mirror this trend: 74 of 105 students or about 71 percent of the students in our School Leadership program are women, and 50 percent of our candidates in our School Business Leader program are women.

- Younger school leaders: In addition to a shift in gender, we are seeing a greater number of educators transitioning to school leadership earlier in their career. According to the same NCES study, the average age of new principals in 2011–2012 was 43.0 years, with experienced principals an average of 11.6 years older (54.6 years old). The difference between the ages of new and experienced public school principals was smaller in 1987–1988, an average of 8.7 years.[4] We have also seen these trends reflected in our program.
- Increasing numbers of school principals: U.S. schools are also seeing more principals assigned to the job than in years past. Specifically, from the 1987–1988 school year to the 2011–2012 school year, the total number of public school principals grew from 103,290 to 115,540, a gain of 12 percent.[5]
- Changing racial demographics of principals: Although principals in U.S. public and private schools are predominantly White, the proportion of White principals decreased between 1987–1988 and 2011–2012 in both public and private schools. During the same time period, the percentage of Black principals did not change significantly, and the percentage of Hispanic principals increased by 4 percentage points from 3 to 7 percent.[6]
- Increasing diversity in student populations in public schools: From the fall 2003 through the fall 2013, the number of White students enrolled in public elementary and secondary schools decreased by almost 3 million. In contrast, the number of Hispanic students enrolled during this period increased by 3.5 million, and since the fall 2002, the percentage of students enrolled in public schools who were Hispanic has exceeded the percentage that were Black.[7] In addition to changes in racial diversity, schools are seeing increased rates of students living in poverty. In the nine-county Rochester area, from where we draw almost all of our students, 19 percent of the children are considered poor, and in the Rochester City School District a staggering 88 percent of the students live in poverty, the second poorest among comparably sized cities in the nation. Rochester is also the fifth-poorest city in the country overall. Black and Hispanic poverty rates in the Nine County Region are 34 percent and 33 percent, respectively, compared to the rate of Whites at 10 percent.[8] However, rural poverty is also an issue in the Nine

County Area, with poverty rates in towns ranging from 2 percent all the way up to 41 percent. Indeed, one in five children in the area are considered poor. In addition, Rochester is the fifth most segregated city in the nation as measured by the Manhattan Institute 2012 Policy Report.[9] These regional data require our students to be aware of the role bias plays in schools, the impact of trauma on students, and how to provide adequate resources for higher-needs students despite limited budgets (i.e., students with disabilities, undocumented students, bilingual and non-native English speakers).

- Adoption of national curriculum standards: The adoption of the Common Core State Standards (CCSS) impacts how schools adjust the way they view both curriculum and instruction, requiring educational leaders to have increased knowledge of CCSS and the associated shifts to instructional practice so they can support teachers through these changes. The statewide adoption of CCSS in New York remains controversial, largely due to its connection to changing state assessments, and has resulted in a statewide movement where parents are opting their children out of these assessments. Significant percentages of students opting out impacts a school's standing with the State Education Department.

- Proposed Changes to Federal Spending: Changes in leadership at the USDOE after the election of 2016 point to a new era of shifting priorities. For example, impending cuts to Title II grants for teacher and principal training, twenty-first-century community learning centers, and teacher quality partnership grants, as well as a shifting focus on public schools of choice, promise new challenges for educational leaders and our program.

- Increased need to collect and use data: The ages of No Child Left Behind (NCLB) and the Every Student Succeeds Act (ESSA) placed student performance in the national spotlight. State education systems responded by placing higher demands on schools to increase student achievement. In New York, schools faced significant changes all in the *same* school year— changing curriculum and changing state assessments—requiring educational leaders to increase their focus on data collection and analysis. While there is uncertainty around accountability measures at the national level, New York currently has no plans to reduce state requirements of schools.

- Increased emphasis on accountability: In addition to changing how students were measured, NCLB and ESSA placed teacher performance in the spotlight, thus impacting teacher evaluation. New York, for example, requires all schools to adopt an Annual Professional Performance Review (APPR) for all certified teaching staff, an initiative that came at the same time as changing assessments and curriculum. Under APPR in New York, teacher evaluation scores were directly linked to student performance on state assessments. All data collected by schools are either published or easily accessible to the public.

- Increased use of technology, both in and out of the classroom: In today's world, technology advances faster than anything else, and educational leaders are expected to consider how to keep schools current with their use of technology despite limited budgets. In addition, social media has changed how quickly and broadly information is shared. Today, school leaders must understand the various forms of social media and the issues associated with them involving parents, students, and staff.
- Teacher and leader shortages, particularly in high-poverty areas: The United States is facing its first teacher shortage since the 1990s, and these shortages are most greatly felt in the areas of Special Education, math, science, and English-language education. According to a 2016 study released by the Learning Policy Institute, the United States experienced a 35 percent decline in enrollment in teacher education programs from 2009 to 2014. In addition, the study showed that in 2014, on average, less than 1 percent of teachers were uncertified in low-minority schools, while four times as many were uncertified in high-minority schools. Teacher attrition—the number of teachers leaving the profession for a variety of reasons—remains high and is the single-biggest contributor to the shortage. Teacher turnover is especially high in poor and disadvantaged schools. The greatest factor cited for teacher attrition is job dissatisfaction; leaders today need to boost and maintain high morale and nurture their staff in support of teacher retention.[10]
- Adoption of National Leadership Standards: Our program recently completed and was accredited through the Council for the Accreditation of Educator Preparation (CAEP), which aligns the Educational Leadership Policy Standards to our assessments. However, new leadership standards are forthcoming in 2018, which will call for more internal assessment revisions in order to maintain accreditation.
- Different types of schools are represented in our program: Our leadership program serves educators from a variety of educational settings, including public, private, charter, nonprofit, prison schools, and regional educational centers/providers. In the past, you did not have to be certified to be a school leader outside of public schools; today, more educational organizations seek leaders who have received specific training and certification, and who have more experienced leadership skills. Our changing student demographics bring a variety of background and experiences to students' thinking about their coursework, and this requires our courses and professors to be prepared to meet these diverse needs.
- Duality of schools: The diversity of our students requires that our course tasks address the leadership issues and skills that transcend all educational settings while also preparing leaders for the specific needs they will face in their future role based on location. For example, we encounter leaders whose school will provide a rigorous International Baccalaureate program,

requiring the leader to support the implementation of programs that prepare students to be global citizens. In contrast, in the same class we might have a student who will lead in a rural school that cannot even offer more than one foreign language or any electives for students. This leads to a greater need for differentiated tasks and experiences, as well as professors who have broad knowledge of the leadership issues in a variety of educational settings.

THE IMPETUS FOR CHANGE

This is an extensive and exhausting list whose impact on our program is monumental. And never before have we felt the need to shift how we prepare future educational leaders. In years past, the belief that "leaders are born, not made" and that only certain people are cut out for educational leadership supported a program that was content driven. In this program, students were taught the nuts and bolts of school management tasks, that is, how to create a budget, hire a teacher, create a schedule, etc. Today, in order to effectively and successfully meet the demands of contemporary education, we must expect our program and its professors and coursework to "move" our students to a leadership mindset so they can be responsive in this ever-changing educational landscape.

As Fullan explains in his book, *The Change Leader* (2011), our students and schools need "change agents" rather than managers of people and things.[11] We share Fullan's belief and propose that *leadership is a mindset*, a "state trait." To do this, our program aims to intentionally prepare future leaders who are metacognitive, critical thinkers and collaborative decision makers. In the specific examples that we present in this chapter, you will see how through redesigning course tasks and structure, as well as overall program goals, we are producing leaders who can think, understand the context of various situations, and use evidence to make both cognitive and metacognitive decisions.

Our work remains in progress; what we share are the beginning stages of this necessary program change and the immediate impact it has had on our students and faculty. Our story tells of how we are embracing what it means to truly be change agents in order to transform our department, our students, and the quality of educational leaders in our community.

Influences for Change

You can't find the answers outside yourself-you have to start inside and look for the best external connections to further develop your own thinking.[12]

The work of Fullan and Hargreaves and others guided and influenced our thinking as we worked to transform our department the past three years to reflect the changes in our field associated with the factors cited in the previous section. We recognized that there were elements of our program, like our internships, that were meeting the needs of most of our students; yet much of the coursework reflected a view of leadership that was managerial and hierarchical—a model based on organizational efficiency and accountability but not reflective of the changing nature of educational organizations and students.

We do not discount the need for educational leaders to "sweat the details" of management; they need to. But we also recognize the need to change our program to emphasize the value and importance of relationship-building and trust, and teaching our future educational leaders to communicate and engage with teachers to collectively reform teaching and learning.[13] We also needed to empower our future leaders to think about the faculty and students that they will be serving the next thirty years. New leaders will be working with a generation of digital native students and faculty. They replace the so-called "analog generation" who grew up with less technology and a greater likelihood of working under hierarchical leadership models. But today's students in our program and the students that they will teach will grow up digitally connected and are already pushing back on issues like the work environment and school schedules associated with an agrarian past. So, in conjunction with this, we recognized that online learning, combined with a focus on critical thinking and metacognition, needed to guide our transformation.

Writers and thinkers in both the field of education and the broader fields of business and social science influenced our transformative work. We found commonalities among and between these writers. For example, in his book *The 8th Habit, From Effectiveness to Greatness* (2004), Stephen Covey writes that leadership involves communicating people's worth and potential to them so clearly that they see it themselves. He goes on to say that leadership should focus on modeling, aligning, and empowering those you lead.[14] And with what he calls knowledge workers (and what are educators if not this?), we must prepare leaders to focus on releasing people's potential and not controlling them.[15] These ideas closely echo those of Daniel Pink (2009) and his research on intrinsic motivation for skilled workers. His ingredients of motivation include the ideas of autonomy through teamwork, mastery, and purpose, or the desire to be involved in something larger.[16] We wanted to change our program to be less a series of courses required by the State of New York, the standards of our discipline, and our CAEP certification process to one in which our students recognized that leaders must be self-directed and self-monitor their attitudes and behaviors. This was a tall task.

In our work, Fullan and Hargreaves have shown our students and us other ways to view leadership and the future of our field. The authors contrast proponents of a business capital model, who view education as a market and teachers and leaders as disposable, flexible, and temporary, with the Professional Capital model which has been adopted by "high performing economies and educational systems around the world."[17] In this model schools and learning institutions are based on trust and communication. We recall the adage in our field that "it is about the students" and, of course, that is true; but we maintain that it is just as much about the adults who are working with generation after generation of those students.

THE EVOLUTION OF OUR THINKING

The work of the National Research Council, How People Learn, and other researchers on the science of learning led Jeff to get a grant and write a book chapter on the development of critical thinking in online and hybrid courses. The purpose of this research was to "investigate, design, and implement rigorous questions, assignments and assessments that would lead to critical thinking in an asynchronous online or hybrid course."[18] This work was based on three assumptions:

1. Technology is not pedagogy. In online learning pedagogical teaching skills and curriculum design are at least as important as technological skills.
2. Learning a complex body of knowledge online requires questions, tasks, and assessments that are designed at multiple levels of a learning taxonomy.
3. More media does not appear to enhance learning; however, asynchronous online communication like discussion boards has been found to lead to more self-reflection and deeper learning.

For this grant we collected data from students in our program on online learning and critical thinking. When asked to describe their experiences in critical thinking and what that construct meant to them, we discovered how much most students wanted to stretch themselves to think at higher levels. A small sample of these data on student responses included:

- A person who thinks critically does not accept information as fact without considering the source of the information and the context in which it appears.
- It wasn't until I examined and researched topics in my Educational Administration coursework that I became aware of the importance of critical thinking and its connection with the writing process.

- The online questions were posed so that critical thinking was needed in order to respond. Sources of class texts, research, or theory were applied to responses in order to support the answers.
- Reading and considering the responses of my peers online increased my desire and ability to think critically.
- Critical thinking prevents me from jumping to erroneous conclusions based on what evidence I hope to see.
- It made me ponder, "Am I engaged in critical thinking?" My thought would be that if you are already wondering, then you probably are because critical thinking takes consideration and metacognition—thinking about thinking.

That last statement was powerful to us because we were both thinking and writing about the relationship between critical thinking and metacognition. Our scholarship informed our practices and program changes. In our research and work we had come to believe that metacognitive approaches to instruction helped our learners take control of their own learning if they:

- Recognize what they understood and when they needed new information;
- Recognize the strategies they need to assess their own understanding;
- Realize the importance of building the individual theories;
- Recognize their intellectual strengths and weaknesses.[19]

Building upon these ideas we started work on an article and conference presentation that served to inform our work. We recognized that our challenge was to design and implement coursework that reflected our belief systems on continuous growth while giving our learners more opportunities to embrace and think about their own growth. We agreed with the work on critical thinking—that while everyone thinks they are doing it, much of their thinking is distorted, uninformed, and prejudiced.[20] We also saw the idea of critical thinking as the thread connecting not only our program but also the student learning standards in the common core curriculum and all professional learning for adults.[21] In our research we revisited the work of Pearson and Gallagher's Gradual Release of Responsibility (GRR) model[22] and completed our own model of Metacognitive Professional Learning[23] that came to guide and inform both our work in the schools and with the students in our Educational Leadership courses (see figure 2.1).

Our model guided us as we redesigned assignments and assessments. Note that at the center of the model is our commitment to focus our students on critical thinking about practice. Branching out from the center are five professional learning practices grounded in GRR.

The Process of Metacognitive Professional Learning

Continuous Formative Assessment that Leads to Metacognition

Gradual Release of
Responsibility

Coaching

Modeling/Think
Aloud

Focus on Critical
Thinking about
Practice

Independent
Application and
Reflection

Professional
Collaboration

Whole Group
Professional
Development/
Training

Figure 2.1. The Process of Metacognitive Professional Learning Model (Donnelly &
Linn, 2014)

We view GRR as a nonlinear approach to professional learning; the important idea in all the practices of our model is the gradual release or scaffolding
of the learning of our students. We know that in our program we have teachers and counselors with anywhere from three to twenty years' experience
in their current positions; they are at very different places in understanding.
Therefore, our professional learning practices are flexible and based on the
needs of the learner, whether it is understanding how to run an effective meeting, learning how to observe teachers, developing a school improvement plan
(SIP), or any of the other competencies we have designed in our program.
The ultimate goal of all coursework and learning experiences is to engage
students in continuous formative assessment of their leadership development
in order to increase metacognition.

Transforming Course Tasks and Activities
to Promote Metacognition

In order to promote critical thinking *within* our courses, we have revised course tasks and assignments. Specifically, we are moving away from the traditional research paper toward relevant, current scenario-based tasks that allow students to apply research and leadership skills to contextual situations they might (and most likely will) encounter in the field.

For example, in our building-level leadership course, students historically selected from a list of current school management topics, conducted research on related best practices, and composed a three- to four-page paper. Most recently, this assignment transformed into a partner-collaborative presentation where students are given one of ten to twelve school managerial scenarios and are asked to present their recommendation to address the scenario based on (1) interviews with acting school leaders and (2) research of best practices (see figure 2.2). Students present their scenario and suggested course of action to their peers and provide a professional bibliography as well as relevant artifacts that can be used for future reference. In this task, students have a chance to not only learn more about how to address specific aspects of building-level management, but to apply what they learned within a specific context. Using their research, students must make decisions by synthesizing what they learned with their own leadership style, and provide a rationale for their decision.

In our School Law course, the professor takes a similar approach, making all assignments scenario based. In this course, students research current New York State laws and regulations, as well as federal laws, and apply them to specific scenarios that a school leader will encounter on any given day (see figure 2.3). In addition, students engage in role-playing scenarios where multiple stakeholders are involved and multiple perspectives need to be considered when applying the law to make decisions (figure 2.4). Again, this approach to learning—an intentional course design focused on promoting critical thinking and metacognitive decision making—shifts the thinking from the professor to the students and prepares educational leaders who can be responsive yet knowledgeable when making decisions.

Another example of how we have transformed our coursework to allow students to think more critically about the work of leading change in schools is our course on Leading Instructional Improvement. In this course, students learn the ins and outs of school improvement planning by assessing their current school/organization using the New York State Diagnostic Tool for School and District Effectiveness (DTSDE) rubric. The New York State Education Department (NYSED) uses the DTSDE rubric to assess and evaluate schools

Maintaining Safe School Facilities

Part I: As AP, you are walking the halls of the school when you hear shouting coming from the main office. As you get closer, you see a man arguing with a staff member. Just as you are getting ready to intervene, the man turns and walks away from the office, toward the classrooms. You try to find out what he needs but he ignores you and keeps walking.

- Describe the emergency action steps/procedures that you put into place immediately.
- What examples of current emergency plan procedures and protocols can you find that represent best practices in similar situations?

Part II: A half-hour before lunch is to be served the sink backs up and sends sewerage water all over the food service area and into the cafeteria. The cafeteria workers refuse to serve the food because of their fear of contamination and the smell in the cafeteria. They call their boss who tells them to leave the area until it is cleaned up and the health inspector checks it out. The sewerage smell is beginning to drift down the corridor into the classrooms. The custodian goes to the area and says that the water is still leaking out and a plumber should be called. He estimates that it will take a few hours to clean up the sewerage and disinfect the area. He says that it would not be ready for the end of the day. Some of the cafeteria workers are complaining of feeling sick to their stomachs. You are concerned about the smell that is beginning to permeate the area.

- Describe the immediate action steps you take in response to this situation.
- Provide examples of food safety codes or regulations, as well as other regulations regarding hygienic conditions in schools that will help guide your decision.

Social Media

You have just been hired as the new principal of a [rural/urban/suburban] K–5 school following the tenure of the previous principal who was the school leader for seventeen years. Your superintendent has asked you to increase your parent and community outreach using current forms of social media.

- Develop a *plan* for how you will use social media to communicate with stakeholders, including the social media platform(s) you will use and how you will use them (i.e., frequency, topics, who will be in charge of messaging, how you will launch these initiatives).
- In addition, be sure to identify *best practices* when using social media as a school leader. You may wish to review your school/district's social media policy as part of your research and share this with your peers.

Figure 2.2. Sample Tasks on Building-Level Leadership

STUDENT TRANSPORTATION: A parent enrolled her first grader in a nonpublic school. The family subsequently lost their house due to a fire and moved into a hotel out of the district. The parents intend to find a new location in the former district. The parents registered the student in the new school district, but expected the former school to provide transportation to the nonpublic school. The former school district refused. The parents appealed the decision. Should the district's denial of transportation be upheld? Why or why not?

DISCIPLINE PENALTY: A child was found in possession of a total of 25 grams of marijuana distributed among thirteen smaller bags. The district proved that the child passed a bag to another student and suspended the student for a full year. Another student found in possession of 25 grams of marijuana was only suspended for two months. The mom of the first child appeals the decision arguing the year suspension is excessive. Should the district suspension of the first child be upheld? Why or why not?

CUSTODY: The mother of a twelve-year-old female student wrote to the school stating that she is now separated from her husband, the student's father and directed that neither the husband/father nor his significant other living with him may visit or pick up the student from school. The mother referred to possible danger to the student from the husband. The mother included a copy of a court order providing her with sole custody and the husband with visitation every other weekend and on Wednesdays and Wednesday nights. The husband arrived to pick up his daughter at the end of school on a Wednesday. The district permitted the student to leave with him, and the mother appealed its action. Should the district have permitted the husband/father to pick up the student? Why or why not?

Figure 2.3. Examples of Brief Scenarios from School Law Course

SCENARIO: The district has brought 3020-a charges against a certified, tenured teacher. The teacher is being charged with misconduct, insubordination, and conduct unbecoming of a teacher. The teacher allegedly engaged in conduct "intimidating a 17-year-old female student into posing for explicit photos in a classroom closet that was used for storage, to have engaged the teen in inappropriate activities including fondling her breasts and genitals as well as posing for the photos under the pretense of attracting college recruiters and employers; encouraged the student to look sexier, and that he had to see more of the scantily clad teen for the supposed college portfolio."

The teacher is a nationally regarded history teacher and is regionally known for his methods and effective teaching, having been praised for his interdisciplinary lessons, use of multimedia in the classroom, and use of brain exercises and memory tools. An overwhelming majority of his students at the predominantly low-income, minority school regularly pass the global history and geography state exams and is a two-time "Teacher of the Year." The Board of Education does not want to settle the case because they want to send a message and because of the high-profile nature of the case.

Group 1: As the assistant superintendent and staff you have analyzed the costs and benefits of proceeding with or settling the case. Prepare a written report and be prepared to explain to the Board (with the assistance of the other cast members) the disciplinary *process*, the legal *issues*, and the *reasons that settling the 3020-a charges is more cost-effective* and preferable than preceding with a hearing and how you would mediate the matter. Submit the written report with Group 2's submission as one document. Present the district's position orally in class session 4.

Group 2: As the district's teacher's representatives, you have analyzed the costs and benefits of proceeding with or settling the case. Prepare a written report and be prepared to present to the teacher (with the assistance of your cast members) the disciplinary process, the legal issues, and the reasons that settling the 3020-a charges is more advantageous than preceding with the hearing and how you would mediate the matter. Submit the written report with Group 1's submission as one document. Present the union's position orally in class session 4.

Cast of Characters: Group 1: for example, superintendent, assistant superintendents for Finance and for Curriculum and Instruction, Human Resources director, principal; Group 2: teacher's union representative from regional office; unit's president; teacher, unit's vice president, others.

Figure 2.4. Examples of Role-Playing Scenarios from School Law Course

across the state that are at risk of closure due to poor performance. Through coursework, students increase their understanding of NYSED criterion for school quality by applying this knowledge to assess their own school and plan for needed improvement. The outcome is a sample SIP—a document that most, if not all, school leaders across New York create prior to each school year whether they are in need of improvement or not (figure 2.5). A quality school improvement planning process is a best practice for all school leaders, and our course embeds students in this decision-making process through an authentic analysis and assessment of their own school. Semester after semester, students report actually implementing their SIP in their school or organization in order to create needed change. This is the ultimate goal of our program, and the need of educational leaders today: educational leaders who can "move" people.

In addition to designing course tasks that require our students to apply their learning to relevant scenarios, our courses intentionally engage students in increasing their self-awareness. For example, in our introductory course, Foundations of Educational Leadership, students take leadership skill inventories and read about multiple theories of and approaches to leadership in order to identify their areas of strength and growth and set metacognitive goals for themselves during their time in the program.

In multiple courses, professors engage students in identifying their personal biases and assumptions in order to think critically about how these impact their leadership decisions. Specifically, students in the 6-credit Hybrid Foundations of Leadership course have to complete at least seven online discussion assignments scored using the Critical Thinking Value Rubric published by the American Association of Colleges and Universities that includes the categories of Explanation, Evidence, Influence of Context and Assumptions, Influence of Student Perspective, and Conclusions.[24] In one assignment students are given readings on poverty and stereotyping, and after reading are asked:

1. Please take the risk to share some of your own stereotypes (or generalizations if you want to use a more comfortable word) with us about the poor or any other group that the article made you think about. Where do you think your views come from and what are the limits of your knowledge about them?
2. Is there anything you can do to change your perspective? Please explain what you can and why it is important in your future as a leader.

These types of tasks are typical of our online assignments throughout the program and align with our program focus on critical thinking and metacognition. We strive to create an online caring community, and recognize that

Specific Indicator	Current Status	Action	Timeline	Resources – Please Name Source	Who's Responsible: Primary Secondary	Evidence of Change Identify Evaluation or Progress Monitoring Tool
SMART Goal: By June 2018, 70% of students in grades 2-6 will be reading on grade level as measured by the Fountas & Pinnell Benchmark assessment.						
Statement of Practice 3.5: Teachers implement a comprehensive system for using formative and summative assessments for strategic short and long-range curriculum planning that involves student reflection, tracking of, and ownership of learning.	a) Teachers are beginning to develop a system to analyze and use data to make curricular decisions.	Grade-level data file: demonstrating multiple measures of student data (exit tickets, anecdotal records, interim and unit benchmarks)	Twice monthly coinciding with data meetings	Common assessments	Teachers Teacher Team Leaders	Alignment of meeting minutes and data file Student performance on benchmark assessment to monitor progress toward goal
	b) Teachers are in the process of developing multiple types of assessments to ensure alignment between curriculum and assessment, or the use of a variety of assessments is inconsistent throughout the school.	Benchmark reading records administered	3-5 times per year, based on grade level and student need	Leveled Literacy Intervention Fountas & Pinnell Assessment system	Grade-level teams AIS Coordinator	Professional Development Plan Walkthrough "look-fors" and conversations about formative assessments
		Professional learning related to formative assessments—using anecdotal records and exit tickets to inform instruction	August 2017 Every other month, thereafter	Guskey EngageNY	Teacher Team Leaders Curriculum Coordinator	Formative assessment data will be demonstrated in student data files
		Teachers will use multiple measures for formative assessment	Daily/Weekly	Guskey EngageNY	All teachers Teacher Team	Walkthrough "look-fors" will show use of formative assessments

Figure 2.5. Excerpt from Student SIP

sometimes people say things to their peers online that they might not say in class. For example, one student wrote of a relative who had been killed in the 9/11 attacks and his struggle not to blame "certain groups because of this" and how "hard it is not to place the blame." Another student wrote of growing up sheltered in a predominantly White middle class community and getting a job in Rochester. In her online entry she shared a reflection from her first day on the job: "I had never been in a room with so many black people before and I was terrified." She went on to say that her initial reaction seems silly now but "the fact was I was completely ignorant." Still another student put themselves into the shoes of a poor Black parent and how it must feel to leave work and money and be called into school for a meeting with an all-White administrative staff.

In our building-level Leadership course, students participate in a one-day shadowing experience of a current school leader who works in a different demographic than their own. For example, a teacher in a suburban elementary school might shadow a principal in an urban high school, or a high school guidance counselor in the city might shadow an elementary principal in a rural school setting. After shadowing the school leader, students reflect on this experience in writing in order to increase their self-awareness and meta-cognitive decision-making abilities. The following questions help to guide this reflection and analysis:

- Identify your biases and assumptions that you bring into your observation experience, for example, high school principals work harder than elementary principals; elementary principals deal with less behavioral issues.
- Based on your observation experience, analyze your biases and assumptions for accuracy. What did you observe that challenges/confirms/extends your previous biases and assumptions?
- Analyze the impact of your biases on assumptions. How will these biases/assumptions affect your role as a school leader? What steps will you take to minimize their impact?

Engaging our students in analysis of their biases and assumptions through-out our program is essential when we think about the changing nature of our schools and students. As noted previously, we are seeing an increase in racial and socioeconomic diversity among students. In the Rochester area alone, our students could obtain a position as a school leader in either an urban school where the population is over 90 percent African-American and Hispanic and over 90 percent Free/Reduced priced lunch (FRPL—a measure of student socioeconomic status in schools), or in a rural school where the student population has a higher rate of FRPL and over 90 percent White with a subgroup of students from migrant farming Latino families. Therefore, the impact of a school leader's biases and assumptions is significant when making decisions and forming relationships.

In another one of our courses, students continue to deepen their self-awareness by engaging in a reflection about their "Signature Presence." By definition, *Signature Presence* is what you specifically bring to your work and play that nobody else brings. When you are authentic, influential, and connected, you exhibit this signature. It is always potent and interdependent and never at the expense of you or the people with whom you interact.[25] Using the questions in a graphic organizer to guide their reflection (figure 2.6), students critically analyze their signature presence in order to (1) better understand their impact on those around them, and (2) intentionally leverage their presence to be more effective in their role. After independent reflection, students are encouraged to ask a critical friend to complete this same graphic organizer, providing feedback about how others perceive their colleague's signature presence. Each semester, students report that this exercise supports their professional growth; not only does it allow individuals to self-identify areas of strength and weakness, but it also allows their trusted colleagues to both confirm and adjust their thinking about the messages they send to others.

Such a task is an excellent example of how we strive to promote meta-cognition in order to develop educational leaders who, through their self-awareness, intentionally harness their strengths to impact student success and who are open to continuous growth and development.

There are other examples similar to these across all courses; these tasks and assignments will continue to evolve as our program-wide understanding and emphasis of our vision, as it aligns with current educational needs, also

---

Imagine someone is observing you exhibiting your signature presence. What will they *see, hear, feel,* and *think* in each of these areas?

- What is your physical presence (body language, stance, energy level)?
- Voice and speech—what words do you use? What is the tone and quality of your voice? How much do you speak (or not)?
- What are you wearing and why?
- Actions—Where do you sit or stand? How do you move around a room? What is your level of focus?

Describe your impact on others when you are exhibiting your signature presence.

Figure 2.6.   Excerpts of Reflection Questions from Signature Presence Activity

evolves. Not only do these tasks demonstrate our program's commitment to our vision—creating leaders who are critical thinkers and metacognitive decision makers—but they also exemplify the understanding and application of quality leadership skills and knowledge in today's schools.

Transforming Course Structure to Promote Metacognition

There is no cookbook full on how to be an educational leader; a principal's first day on the job can bring any number of situations for which a person is not prepared. Just like newly certified doctors, educational leaders jump right into the thick of their work on day one. It's impossible to know exactly what it means to run a school without actually doing the job. This is why we, in addition to changing the way we engaged our students within courses, also made several changes to how courses are structured to intentionally increase how students participate in relevant and realistic field experiences.

In their final two semesters in our program, students take two courses—Central Office and Internship—that place them directly into the field working with current school and district leaders. In the Central Office course students must be prepared to bridge the gap between the inner workings of individual buildings and the broader context of the entire school district or educational organization. A major assignment in the course is for groups of students to complete a project for a school district in the region and, if applicable, present the results of that project to a Board of Education, Administrative Cabinet, or other stakeholder group associated with the school district. Past projects have looked at issues like: Advanced Placement courses in high school, more effective means of funding food service, middle school algebra, and scheduling counseling programs. These are real issues that help students understand the interactions and strategies needed to serve in a central office position and aid the district in a study that they may not have the resources to complete.

Internship is the intersection of all of the skills, experience, and training that students have learned till date in the program, and is an experience that is as close to being a full-time educational leader as possible in a situation where the student is not actually hired as an administrator. In fact the student, at this point in the program, is qualified for a Certificate of Internship (issued by the NYSED) allowing a student to serve in an administrative position that would normally require certification. During this individualized course, each student works with a full-time building-level or central office administrator (mentor) for forty hours per week over the course of seven weeks in accomplishing administrative tasks. The Internship offers opportunities for more holistic tasks, that is, staff development over a semester, budget development from beginning to end, or recruitment and hiring of personnel. One objective common to all students during the Internship is the further refinement of job-seeking skills (investigating a vacancy, writing a cover letter, writing a resume, and interviewing).

In addition to their field placement, students participate in three seminars throughout the semester. The purpose of the seminars is to provide students with additional shared learning experiences and to prepare them for graduation and certification. To increase metacognition during their internship, we use the seminar to promote collaboration and critical thinking around key leadership issues. For example, we recently added a workshop to our first seminar on "Having Difficult Conversations" where students role-play specific scenarios that require skillful and courageous communication with various school and district stakeholders. At times, we use real scenarios in which students have found themselves in order to share the learning from one student's experience with others. In second seminar, students participate in collaborative conversations about their field experiences, using questions like those below to guide their thinking:

- What's one thing that you've done (i.e., a completed task, an action/reaction to a situation, or a decision you made) that surprised you the most?
- What's one task that you've completed that you didn't know how to do? What did you learn about yourself by working on this task?
- What projects are you currently working on? Explain one thing you are currently doing and how you are making decisions in order to complete this task.
- Tell about a time when you felt overwhelmed by the job in front of you. How did you handle these feelings?
- How are you making time for yourself and your self-care during your full-time internship?

By intentionally posing questions that require students to reflect critically about their developing leadership practice, we are creating metacognitive leaders who will hopefully continue this reflective practice after graduation.

Transforming Program Structure to Promote Metacognition

Our program is unique because it is the only post-Master's program at our college. In New York, Educational Administration is a Certificate of Advanced Study that students can earn in either or both School Building Leadership or School District Leadership. Most of the students enrolled in our program have served as teachers or counselors for a number of years. They have families, jobs, and numerous responsibilities. In the past, upon entry into the program students committed to attend class from 5:00 to 9:00 on Fridays and 9:00 to 4:30 on Saturdays after having worked all week in schools. Over the years students who lived in outlying areas had grudgingly stayed overnight at a hotel. Hence the decision to turn our program into a hybrid was at first a practical one. We wanted to eliminate the Friday night classes. As former principals and teachers we both remember how tired we were at 17:00 on Friday; that model did not make sense to us. But, in addition, as we researched online learning, we found that transitioning into a hybrid program not only had practical benefits but also had the potential to lead to deeper thinking.

Jeff started his research by reading a meta-analysis by the USDOE and was surprised to find that students in online courses performed modestly better than those receiving face-to-face instruction.[26] The authors of the report also suggested that the strongest online coursework could prompt students to reflect on their levels of understanding the content. This indicated that well-designed online prompts and questions could lead to metacognition. Other findings in the meta-analysis indicated that online education had potential for creating engaging content and processes. Then Jeff looked at the work of Noddings and the idea of creating caring communities within the context of hybrid coursework and found that caring classroom communities include receiving and responding to other's perspectives.[27] He saw parallels to the work we were doing on metacognition. So together we closed the circle. If we offered the best of both worlds—face-to-face meetings on Saturdays with quality online components to replace the long weekends—then we would create an environment for our students that was supportive, trusting, and caring with the added bonus of leading to metacognition.

REFLECTIONS ON OUR LEARNING

When you try to make change, you will most certainly experience challenges, and we have our share of them. This year as we made more change than in years past, we noticed specific things that serve as obstacles to consistency across our program and the success of all students.

- It is difficult to "move" people because they do not want to recognize their biases and stereotypes and the impact these have on their practice. Despite our best efforts to promote critical thinking and metacognition, we experience some hesitance when it comes to reflecting about bias. Connected to this, it's easier to give students the "cookbook" rather than create cognitive dissonance; not all students are ready, or willing, for this level of critical thinking.
- As a state university, we rely greatly on adjunct professors, making it challenging to find consistent faculty who are aligned with our philosophy. We

work hard to find highly qualified faculty who are willing to collaborate around course planning, and make investing in human capital a priority.

- Since ours is a postgraduate program, our students are full-time educational organization employees who are busy. Therefore, we see a variance in the level of commitment to coursework, making it hard to assess each student's readiness to be a leader.
- There are students entering our program who are not ready to be educational leaders. In New York, candidates only need one year of successful teaching experience to apply. However, education programs are often viewed as "cash cows." As the college struggles with low enrollment numbers, this impacts the pressure on and expectation of schools of education to keep enrollment numbers up. Rather than selectively screen applicants they self-select their way into our program.

In working to address these obstacles and challenges, we learned that in the face of such adversity, three things remain constant.

RELATIONSHIPS MATTER. Students will not allow themselves to be open to sharing their critical self-reflection around their growth and development of a leadership mindset without trust in the program and our professors. First, we demonstrate competence in our work; we are knowledgeable about our content, organized in our course design, and prepared. Second, we model the same level of critical thinking and metacognition that we encourage in our students. In sharing our own professional stories, we are able to candidly discuss how we grew as leaders through both successes and failures. Third, we take a personal approach when working with all of our students. We take the time to get to know students and their interests, both personal and professional, and allow for considerable collaboration among students so they, too, value the relationships they form among their peers.

A GROWTH MINDSET OF OUR STUDENTS IS A MUST. Our students progress through stages in their development of a leadership mindset. Historically, most students shift their mindset halfway through the program from that of a teacher to that of a leader; it is obvious when they start to view themselves as leaders. We have learned to be patient with our students, recognizing that each student grows at a different rate. For example, we allow students to resubmit assignments, stressing that each task is about the learning rather than the grade. We scaffold learning by chunking course tasks and providing exemplars, as needed. We also require peer review and response of student written reflections and journals to allow students to learn from and with each other rather than only receiving feedback from course professors. In our patience and belief that all students can learn, we have seen students progress from being timid, fixed in their thinking, and/or lax with their schoolwork into assertive, systems thinkers who demonstrate pride in their work. We have also been able to support students in finding the professional path that's right for them. The challenge for us is how to maintain a growth mindset even of those students who consistently display a lack of leadership mindset.

HONEST FEEDBACK IS A GIFT. We have to give our students honest, critical feedback of their growth and performance, including group processes in the courses, performance in on-site experiences, and/or readiness for a school leadership position. To do this, we take the time to respond thoroughly to student work; we ask questions to push thinking and provide direct comments when student work is not accurate or complete. Often, we engage in difficult conversations with our students about their performance and its impact, and we view these conversations as opportunities for professional growth. While in our program, students have the opportunity to make mistakes that don't yet impact the future students in their schools.

CONCLUSION

Just as we want our students to be metacognitive, we, too, are metacognitive thinkers who reflect on our own practices and consistently think about how to improve the quality of our program. And we have many more things we hope to accomplish in the next two to three years. Below is a list of actions that outline some of our long-range action items.

- Formation of an Advisory Board: We gathered a group of ten local educational leaders, some of whom are program graduates, to ensure that our assignments and tasks are relevant and current, and to create contacts in local schools and districts for our interns. Our goal is to continue to meet with this board three times each academic year in support of program goals and initiatives.
- Partnership with Brockport Central School District: This year, our department partnered with the school district in our college town to address issues related to poverty and education. In April 2017, the district will host a poverty conference for schools across the region, and Jeff will serve as one of the presenters.
- Beginning stages of forming a relationship with a Rochester city school: We are working closely with the principal of one elementary school to help support her with specific challenges and needs. Currently, we made a commitment to place one intern there each summer to help with summer programs. This intern will have specific skills related to urban school leadership, literacy instruction, and special education, and will receive additional on-site leadership coaching from one of our professors to ensure quality and effectiveness.

- Implementation of a Teacher Leadership certification program: In the fall of 2016, we launched our Teacher Leadership program, a 12-credit certification course of study for students who want to investigate educational leadership without making a commitment to the full program, yet with the opportunity for a seamless transfer into the Educational Leadership program. This program supports our commitment to a capacity building model of educational leadership grounded in professional capital.

We recognize that our work is in progress; we still have much we want to accomplish to transform our program. We want to make sure that we continue to "move" our students to being metacognitive leaders. To do this, we are certain that underlying all of our goals is our commitment to creating critical thinkers through cognitive dissonance.

Interviews

"Light bulb moments" are often seen as being serendipitous and fleeting. I hope that the following interview questions and answers deepen understanding about how these moments can be cultivated and sustained. The "Light Bulb Moment Worksheet" (appendix) offers a framework for stimulating transformation at your college or university.

Changing the Light Bulb

David: *How many academics does it take to change a light bulb?*

Jeff: (Laughter) I guess in our department only one or two because that's all we have.

Heather: Jeff really got the momentum going, really started the transformation, and I feel really honored to be a partner now to help keep the momentum going and really help to make that change more throughout all of the classes.

Question for Reader Reflection

What could be done to help your team members improve their ability to lead and follow one another to meet shared goals?

Change Agency

David: *How has your life prepared you to be a change agent?*

Heather: What put me in perspective to this next chapter of my career [higher education] is when I was a principal for 18 months at a charter school here in Rochester. I took that job knowing that it was going to be a big step for me, a stretch for me, a big learning curve for me. But because I really believe in providing quality and equitable education for our children—and not having the ability to be as successful in that role because of things that were out of my control and that bureaucracy that we had to navigate, and turning 40 at the same time [put things in perspective]—I made a promise to myself to never move forward in this career without equity being at the center. And so that really provided me the momentum that I needed to be the change agent.

And Jeff took the chance on me in this position as an assistant professor with him to allow me to continue to impact where leaders are put into schools. . . . And if I can impact these future leaders then this is great. This is a way for me to continue to make sure that students are getting the quality of education that they deserve.

Jeff: I think that at every step of the way of your professional growth there are people that have [enough] confidence in you to say, "You know you can do this." You know even as far as going back for an advanced degree, whether it's a master's degree or a PhD, at some point there was somebody that said—or you say to yourself—"Oh, I'm not PhD material." And [when] you look around at some of the teachers that you've had, you go, "yeah, you know what, I'm as good a teacher as that person." So I think that mentors along the way who encourage you make a difference.

Question for Reader Reflection

How can mentors and mentees be cultivated to transmit the art of change agency?

Advice

David: What advice do you have for others who want to transform higher education?

Heather: Knowing your moral purpose is I think what's really important. What is your vision? That should be what guides you. I think very often, rather than starting internally with our moral purpose, we're impacted by something outside of us. And when something so outside of us drives us it's very hard for us to persist when we hit those barriers . . . it's harder to pull yourself out of a discouraging situation when you're trying to make change. Know what your purpose is so that you can stay true to yourself throughout the change process.

Jeff: You know, you've got to let people know why it's important and then you've got to let people know what outcomes you desire. So if for example, we're changing our courses and saying we are going to develop—at the center of our courses—leaders that are critical thinkers and decision makers [it has to be clear]: why is that important; this is the outcome we desire. People need to know that you believe that it's important and you need to give them your reasoning; if you do that you can move people along very early on.

Question for Reader Reflection

What is the moral purpose of your initiative and how could that be communicated to build understanding?

NOTES

1 Michael Fullan, *Change Leader: Learning to Do What Matters Most* (New York: Jossey Bass, 2011): 23.

2 "The Condition of Education." Last updated May 2016. https://nces.ed.gov/programs/coe/indicator_cge.asp

3 "The Condition of Education."

4 "The Condition of Education."

5 "The Condition of Education."

6 "The Condition of Education."

7 "The Condition of Education."

8 "Poverty and the Concentration of Poverty in the Nine-County Greater Rochester Area." Updated 2013. www.racf.org

9 "Poverty and the Concentration of Poverty in the Nine-County Greater Rochester Area."

10 Leib Sutcher et al., "A Coming Crisis in Teaching? Teacher Supply, Demand and Shortages in the U.S." Learning Policy Institute, 2016.

11 Fullan, *Change Leader*.

12 Fullan, *Change Leader*, xii.

13 Carrie Leona, "The Missing Link in School Reform." *Stanford Social Innovation Review*. Fall (2011): 1–11; Andy Hargreaves and Michael Fullan, *Professional Capital: Transforming Teaching in Every School* (New York: Teachers College Press, 2012).

14 Stephen Covey, *The 8th Habit: From Effectiveness to Greatness* (New York: Free Press, 2004).

15 Covey, *The 8th Habit: From Effectiveness to Greatness*.

16 Daniel Pink, *Drive: The Surprising Truth about What Motivates Us* (New York: Riverhead Books, 2009).

17 Hargreaves & Fullan, *Professional Capital*, 2.

18 Jeff Linn, "Using a Hybrid Instructional Model to Develop Critical Thinking Skills for Candidates in a Course on Becoming a Principal," in *Critical Thinking for College Learners: Blended and Online Activities in Multiple Disciplines*, Ed. Lynae E. Warren (Brockport: Emerson & Brockway, 2015), 32.

19 National Research Council. *How People Learn: Brain, Mind, Experience, and School* (Washington, DC: National Academy Press, 2000).

20 Richard Paul and Linda Elder. *Critical Thinking—Concepts & Tools* (Tomales, CA: Foundation for Critical Thinking, 2014).

21 Heather Donnelly and Jeff Linn, "Critical Thinking Skills Fire Up Teacher Learning," *Journal of Staff Development* 35 (2014): 40–44.

22 David P. Pearson and Margaret Gallagher, "The Instruction of Reading Comprehension." *Contemporary Educational Psychology* 8 (1983): 317–344.

23 Donnelly and Linn, "Critical Thinking Skills Fire Up Teacher Learning," 2014.

24 Association of American Colleges and Universities. Critical Thinking VALUE Rubric, 2010. http://www.aacu.org/value/rubrics/critical

25 Mary Beth O'Neill, *Executive Coaching with Backbone and Heart: A Systems Approach to Engaging Leaders with Their Challenges* (San Francisco: Jossey-Bass, 2000).

26 Barbara Means et al., "Evaluation of Evidence Based Practices in Online Learning: A meta-Analysis and Review of Online Learning Studies" (U.S. Department of Education: Office of Planning, Evaluation, and Policy Development, Policy and Program Studies Service, 2010). http://www2.ed.gov/rschstat/eval/tech/evidence-based-practices/finalreport.pdf

27 Nel Noddings, *Caring: A Relational Approach to Ethics and Moral Education. 2nd Edition* (Berkeley: University of California Press, 2013).

PROFESSIONAL RESOURCES

Association of American Colleges and Universities. (2010). Critical thinking VALUE rubric, http://www.aacu.org/value/rubrics/critical

Council for Accreditation for Educator Preparation. http://caepnet.org/accreditation/caep-accreditation/spa-standards-and-report-forms/elcc

Covey, S. (1989). *The Seven Habits of Highly Effective People.* New York, NY: Free Press.

Covey, S. (2004). *The 8th Habit: From Effectiveness to Greatness.* New York, NY: Free Press.

Donnelly, H., & Linn, J. (2014). Critical thinking skills fire up teacher learning. *Journal of Staff Development, 35,* 40–44.

Fullan, M. (2011). *Change leader: Learning to do what matters most.* San Francisco, CA: Jossey-Bass.

Hargreaves, A., & Fullan, M. (2012). *Professional capital: Transforming teaching in every school.* New York, NY: Teachers College Press.

Hill, J., Ottem, R., & DeRoche, J. (2016). *Trends in public and private school principal demographics and qualifications: 1987–88 to 2011–12.* Washington, DC: United States Department of Education.

Leona, C. (2011). The missing link in school reform. *Stanford Social Innovation Review,* Fall: 1–11.

Linn, J. (2015). Using a hybrid instructional model to develop critical thinking skills for candidates in a course on becoming a principal. In L. E. Warren (Ed.), *Critical thinking for college learners: Blended and online activities in multiple disciplines,* pp. 31–56. Brockport: Emerson & Brockway.

Means, B., Toyama, Y., Murphy R., Baika, M., & Jones, K. (2010). *Evaluation of evidence based practices in online learning: A meta-analysis and review of online learning studies*. U.S. Department of Education: Office of Planning, Evaluation, and Policy Development, Policy and Program Studies Service. Retrieved from http://www2.ed.gov/rschstat/eval/tech/evidence-based-practices/finalreport.pdf

National Center for Education Statistics. (2016). *The condition of education*. Retrieved from https://nces.ed.gov/programs/coe/indicator_cge.asp

National Research Council. (2000). *How people learn: Brain, mind, experience, and school*. Washington, DC: National Academy Press.

Noddings, N. (2013). *Caring: A relational approach to ethics and moral education* (2nd ed.). Berkeley, CA: University of California Press.

O'Neill, M. (2000). *Executive coaching with backbone and heart: A systems approach to engaging leaders with their challenges*. San Francisco, CA: Jossey-Bass.

Paul, R., & Elder, L. (2014). *Critical thinking—Concepts & tools*. Tomales, CA: Foundation for Critical Thinking.

Pearson, P. D., & Gallagher, M. (1983). The instruction of reading comprehension. *Contemporary Educational Psychology, 8*: 317–344.

Pink, D. (2009). *Drive: The surprising truth about what motivates us*. New York, NY: Riverhead Books.

Pink, D. (2012). *To sell is human: The surprising truth about moving others*. New York, NY: Riverhead Books.

Sutcher, L., Darling-Hammond, L., & Carver-Thomas, D. (2016). *A coming crisis in teaching? Teacher supply, demand and shortages in the U.S.* Learning Policy Institute. Retrieved from https://learningpolicyinstitute.org/sites/default/files/product-files/A_Coming_Crisis_in_Teaching_REPORT.pdf

The Rochester Area Community Foundation. (2013). *Poverty and the concentration of poverty in the nine-county Greater Rochester Area*. Retrieved from www.racf.org

Chapter 3

Aligning Assessment and Instruction

Dr. Imani Akin and Dr. Crystal Neumann

American College of Education, Indiana

How many academics does it take to change a light bulb?

3 or More

In this chapter Dr. Crystal Neumann, chair of the Leadership Department, and Dr. Imani Akin, academic curriculum director, discuss how they worked to align instruction and assessment at the American College of Education. I was thankful to learn about the "ah-ha moments" that occurred during the writing of their chapter.

Imani: *Writing the piece was like a reflection. I started looking at the numbers and Crystal goes "wait, I didn't know it had grown like this!" We [reflected] on exactly what she had built and what I had the opportunity to help her build to this point.*

Crystal: *You go through day-by-day, you're so busy. You need to get things done. You have e-mails to answer, people to get back to, and there's just not enough time in the day for a quick reflection. And I think that [writing the] chapter has allowed me to really think about what I try to do as a change agent, because I think we're still . . . so fast paced here that we're just building one block right in front of the other and building that pathway for others.*

But sometimes we just need to take a look behind ourselves and realize, "oh my gosh, look at all we've built." So for me that's helped me personally to think about the things that we've done professionally. I think it helps to see the things that we've done correctly as well as anything else that we might've needed to alter or tweak a little bit.

INTRODUCTION

Review of assessment and instruction practices is critical for teaching and learning within higher education. Writing as a form of communication is key in an online learning environment. This chapter addresses faculty and administrative experiences in aligning assessment and instruction of writing in higher education within the context of constant change and supporting student needs.

BACKGROUND AND CHALLENGES

The American College of Education is a fully accredited online college offering programs at the master's level and doctoral level, as well as certificates in education. The bachelor's program was just introduced in April 2017. The American College of Education exists to improve education across the globe. Incorporated in 2005, the college has been accredited by the Higher Learning Commission since 2006. The college mission and vision statement aligns with the core values, goals, and objectives of ensuring and maintaining accountability, affordability, accessibility, technology, innovation, ethics (integrity), and diversity. The mission of the American College of Education is to deliver high-quality affordable and accessible online programs grounded in evidence-based content and relevant application preparing students to lead, serve, and achieve personal and professional goals in diverse, evolving communities (ACE, 2017). With a vision to be a significant presence in higher education by providing high value, innovative, and impactful programming, the American College of Education prepares students to become leaders in their field.

Doctorate degrees within the American College of Education include the Education Specialist (EdS) and Doctorate of Education (EdD). The mission of the EdS and EdD program is to enhance the skills of current school leaders and produce future leaders of education. In addition to developing programs to produce and support leaders in education, the American College of Education seeks to provide support to students needing supplementary instruction in noncontent areas.

The student population in higher education has changed from the selective few to a larger and diverse population of students (Badenhorst, Moloney, Rosales, Dyer, & Ru, 2015). Beyond students whose parents or sibling attended similar or same schools, current student populations include first-generation students, students from working-class backgrounds, students who are tech savvy and those who may not be tech savvy. A wide range of students enrolled in higher education calls for broader content to address varying needs and levels of support. Additional and supplemental courses are necessary to accommodate a diverse student population.

Student writing in higher education is a prominent issue (Cotterall, 2011; Lillis & Turner, 2001). Writing instruction is often implicit in the course programs and part of the hidden curriculum of learning. Some students will improve their writing skills through observation of the writing of others. Other students will require explicit instruction in writing. As an online learning environment, the American College of Education realizes the necessity for successful communication through writing. The ability to communicate in multiple forms is a critical skill for leadership. The online learning environment provides opportunities to practice and enhance writing skills through chats, course discussions, written assignments, and projects.

As the student population changes, change within the educational institution is necessary. Change may occur in multiple areas or layers within schools. School policies, practices, and faculty adjustments in teaching practices will require evaluation, revision, and change. Lewin's Change Model aligned with action research can address issues and support transcending to next level status. The year 2016 included significant growth in the educational specialist and doctoral degree programs. Student enrollment increased by 537 percent since the first program started in 2013. The program grew by 150 percent from 2015 to 2016. Staff increased from four full-time staff and core faculty in 2015 (thirteen part-time faculty) to seven full-time staff and core faculty in 2016 (with twenty-one part-time faculty). Changes in faculty and staff occurred because of termination as well as new hires, to include talent which would better align with the needs of the doctoral program students. Current levels of support from the American College of Education Writing Center include supplementary materials and one-on-one assistance in addressing concerns. The one-on-one assistance is prompted through instructor referrals to the Office of Academic Excellence—a form of action research that emerged to address student writing began in the fall of 2016.

Doctoral faculty identified student writing skills to be a major barrier of success within the program. Faculty of the Education Specialist and Education Doctoral degree program agreed to the need for improved quality of student writing and that improvement in student writing would occur with consistent processes for writing assignments. The challenge was to decide how to address the issue of student writing. Doctoral faculty took the initiative to create supplemental materials such as academic writing tips, resource pages, and students were directed to external videos for support. Several meetings centered around a template with ideas for developing a course.

TEACHING AND LEARNING: AMERICAN COLLEGE OF EDUCATION

Course Development Ideas to Support Student Writing

Topic/Content	Objective	Student Needs
Electronic References	Student will understand and apply APA Reference elements and formatting	APA References
Planning Outline	Student will plan to write using a prompt and develop a structure	Addressing the prompts Focus Heading Intro and Con
Evidence	Student will implement resources to support assertions	Research Scholarly articles Implementing resources plagiarism citations
Generating content Drafting	Student will demonstrate writing skills synthesizing and developing counter arguments and adding alternative views	Quotes Synthesize the Readings Counter argument Alternative view Succinct
Meeting the Academic Writing Standards	Student will develop a doctoral-level paper	Running head Title page Formatting Paragraph size Active and passive voice

Discussion around a proactive approach to supporting students' writing included:

- A decrease in faculty hours spent working with students to meet writing standards
- The need for students to achieve greater progression and success in the program
- Reduced levels of anxiety and frustration for faculty and students
- Greater student efficacy

Dickens and Watkins (1999) posited educators depend on data to support changes to enhance teaching and learning. Lewin's action research model involves a cyclical process of five actions of analysis, planning, acting, observing, and reflecting, useful for data driven instruction. A doctoral instructional faculty member, with department chair approval, began to develop a writing course template based on observations of student writing needs within the courses. The department chair directed the doctoral instructional faculty to share the template with core faculty members who expressed concerns about student writing. The department chair decided to include the writing table during a leadership meeting for feedback. Three meetings with faculty and administration from other departments included a thorough discussion of the writing course template and student support for writing. New knowledge of a course regarding APA writing style was shared with the doctoral instructional faculty member. A discussion regarding legal and policy issues was part of the final meeting before the template was forwarded to administration.

Ongoing changes to support student writing impact and involve various departments, the department of student services, changes to the academic writing center resources, and accountability of doctoral faculty. Sometimes agendas collide as departments address the needs of different programs. In *Changing Minds—The Art and Science of Changing Our Own and Other People's Minds,* Dr. Howard Gardner addressed leadership efforts of change within institutions. The effectiveness of the narrative of change and how the change is conveyed is critical (Gardner, 2006). Getting to an agreement and approval for a writing course for the doctoral program is a work in progress.

CHANGE INITIATIVE

The American College of Education Office of Regulatory Affairs and Compliance provided leadership with an assessment report of student learning outcomes with multiple initiatives to support student learning. Examples of actions planned within the college include increased targets for student mastery of APA format for many of the master's programs in 2016. Specifically, the goal was for 80 percent of the students to average 85 percent or better in scholarly writing and composition (American College of Education, 2016). Changes and revisions to some courses in which the student mastery was not met included integrating links to resources, to supplement the learning and assist students with APA formatting and graduate-level writing. Faculty and staff collaborated to choose additional supplements to address student writing gaps, feedback specific to student writing, and writing resources.

A critical initiative for the Education Specialist and Doctoral program in 2017 is to support student writing (American College of Education, 2016).

The development of a writing course continues to be part of the discussion, as well as gaining consensus and consistency among faculty, staff, and students about standards for writing. The initiative is affecting current policy and processes within our institution.

Excessive amounts of time are spent in the courses for faculty providing constructive and corrective feedback. Some students will reach the end of the chosen programs without mastering the many writing components, such as APA-recommended writing style. Current process in which student writing progresses at the doctoral level occurs through implicit learning such as observation or other invisible dimensions. Unresponsiveness to feedback can be eliminated through explicit instruction. The doctoral writing course will support students who require additional instruction in meeting doctoral-level academic writing standards. Students will receive direct instruction on scholarly writing.

SUCCESSES AND OBSTACLES

Obstacles to improving student writing include consistency in faculty feedback on student writing. Successes have occurred in developing professional learning communities to address student writing. Faculty will submit tips and ideas to add to the faculty meeting agenda and for discussion and building of rapport around student issues. Another obstacle addressed by one faculty member is the perception of inertia regarding student writing. The faculty communicated, "We need to address this issue to avoid faculty burnout."

Successes include reviewing and enhancing some admissions processes. Gardner (2006) revealed the experience of successful new leaders to not immediately address or blame faculty skills to preserve relationships. Gardner found successful strategies in raising the school standards included raising the criteria for admissions and instituting faculty rewards. Recognition of the role of accountability and consistency in faculty feedback is key to student progress. Addressing the admissions process and faculty accountability is part of the action research plan. Successes include beginning the development of the writing course and obstacles would be faculty resisting change. The development of the writing course continued to emerge through the observation of student needs. Achievement of student success in writing is dependent on faculty's active participation and observation.

One rebuttal toward adding the writing course was the increase in cost of tuition. As with any course development an instructor is necessary. The college strives for affordability, keeping the faculty member's salary in mind, and embracing the philosophy of *teacher-made* in course development and instruction such as "By the Teacher for the Teacher." Consideration of affordability indicates the course may save the student money in the long run. For example, if students are provided with the tools to correct writing deficiencies and understand actions needed to improve, students can save money on retaking courses, APA editors, or prolonged dissertation development due to writing deficits. Improvement in writing can increase students' self-esteem and confidence to continue within the education specialist and doctoral programs. A writing course can result in faculty and student efficacy, serving as a catalyst for forward movement in dissertation development while decreasing the possibility of ABD (All But Dissertation).

Plans for the doctoral writing course include providing resources to serve as learning objects in the course. Learning activities include readings, interactive activities, and tutorials. Discussion of plans for student selection for this course includes consideration of the results of a writing assessment in the five-week course, LEAD6001: Introduction to Advanced Graduate Study, in which students who receive a "C" or lower grade will be eligible. One plan includes calls for students to begin writing assessment in week three and have the opportunity to implement instructor feedback into a rewrite in week four. Faculty in other courses may also recommend students take the writing course with evidence of the student's work.

Communication

It can be difficult to change the organizational mindset when individual responses include, "But we've always done it this way." Transitioning through change is essential for organizational harmony, and it is also crucial for the change to take place. Because change is inevitable in the workplace, leaders must help faculty, staff, and students to face the unknown rather than ignore the uncertainties. Effective managers resolve and embrace change and possess social and communication skills to listen to staff members and dare to implement suggestions at all levels.

Clear and consistent communication from leadership is especially helpful when organizations are going through change. Employees can be resistant to change. Faculty frustration can lead to negativity, complaints, and an unpleasant working environment. Scott and Garland (2007) argued resistance to change is an emotional condition. Frustration and anxiety may be used and felt by those who resist change due to confusion and misunderstanding of the bigger picture (Scott & Garland, 2007). Dealing with such changes would require a leader who understands the discomfort of change and how to communicate in such a way that the change no longer seems scary. Leaders have a significant role in managing communication, changing acceptance, and overcoming obstacles (Kulkarni, 2016).

To support changes within the doctoral program, weekly meetings were scheduled with full-time faculty and staff for discussions on the writing levels of doctoral students. Discussions during the meetings revealed some students were not receiving effective and specific feedback, while some students received extensive feedback, and some students were not responsive to faculty feedback. Instructors who offered extensive feedback to students received many complaints from students because students were being pushed out of their comfort zone. Students also complained, "How can I be this off when my last instructor didn't tell me anything I was doing was wrong?"

One focus point of the doctoral program is to encourage students to embrace the progression of building and enhancing their scholarly writing skills. Review of practices reveals challenges to maintaining this focus point without faculty consistency in providing effective feedback. Classroom observations and discussions with adjunct faculty took place to help keep faculty performance consistent. Three feedback groups emerged during this process. In Group 1, faculty took the discussions to heart and implemented more feedback. Other faculty in Group 2 were slower to implement feedback, but took a "slowly but surely" approach. There were other faculty in Group 3 who were more resistant and did not change the approach.

All groups received information and coaching on the importance of staying consistent. The department chair discussed how consistent and inconsistent actions of faculty impacted students such as how some students were less prepared in comparison to peers who received extensive feedback, to apply for doctoral candidacy. There was also discussion on students who were less willing to accept feedback from instructors who were trying to help them understand the gaps in their research and academic writing. The running theme of these conversations centered on a shared vision among all faculty.

Faculty and staff may, sometimes, feel there is overcommunication. Leaders who may be perceived as overcommunicating can be considered successful, as being overly informed is much better than being underinformed. Team huddles or weekly meetings are useful to keeping the shared vision alive and deliver timely information. Such team management also promotes collective decision making and empowers others to offer input. Use of these formats can generate ideas around student writing and documentation. Fostering huddles within the workplace is also effective team building practice and can promote productivity (Frank, 2011). When leaders undercommunicate, employees may become resistant to change. The department chair found faculty preferred a communication style of transparency from change agents. Faculty, staff, and students preferred to be informed through the changes and transition processes.

Consideration of the recipients of communication is important. A communications instructor can be credited for initiating a paradigm shift in the thinking of the department regarding how the chair communicated with others. The former communications instructor told the department chair that no matter how well you try to explain something, the person you are explaining to may not always understand 100 percent of the message. The lack of understanding has nothing to do with the listener not listening, this was because no two people have the exact same personal beliefs, biases, upbringings, experiences, and so forth. The communication instructor demonstrated this through an exercise. In the demonstration session, one person looked at a picture and explained how to draw the picture to the others in the session. Afterward, everyone shared their drawing, and the person who gave the directions for drawing explained what each person's drawing revealed. Most of the pictures were vastly different. This concrete example reminds the department chair to provide a variety of detailed explanations and communication opportunities to support change initiatives.

Turning Concerns into Resolutions

Emotional intelligence is another important skill set leaders can use to help faculty, staff, and students accept changes (Di Fabio, Bernaud, & Loarer, 2014), setting a positive tone for candor and trust through individual dialogue and conversations. It is easier for faculty, staff, and students to move through the change when leaders communicate and model the process. Transparency eliminates surprises and potential anxiety, which may arise with changes. Leaders with high emotional intelligence will recognize faculty hesitancy and concerns, as well as help faculty and staff accept the changes.

One adjunct faculty discussed concerns with regard to providing feedback because of the amount of time involved, although this is the job of faculty. The department chair seized the opportunity to diminish faculty concerns and ask for ideas to discuss ways to offset the amount of time spent. It was clear the faculty's emotions were involved by bringing what should have been obvious and may have been obvious at another time. It was important to realize time involved with providing feedback was something other instructors were worried about, and did not verbalize. This concern was also discussed with full-time faculty and staff to discuss this time involved providing feedback and other challenges instructors might have. By the end of the meeting, there were several resolutions discussed, which included developing faculty resources. One main idea was to design a resource with common and frequent APA errors found in student papers. One plan was for the resource document to be used by all faculty to copy, paste, and include into the student's paper. The resource document would ensure accurate information and keep faculty consistent in the delivery of feedback, particularly for rules about APA. The information was posted in a portion of the Learning Management System (LMS), in which only faculty have access.

ORGANIZATIONAL CULTURE AND LESSONS LEARNED

Leaders have an opportunity to impact the culture of organizations. Establishing a culture of learning supports change and can help propel ideas forward.

It is important to remember to listen to faculty, staff, and students in the organization. There are some faculty, staff, and students who may not address issues or make suggestions. Fortunately, some faculty will persist in bringing issues to the forefront such as in the case of the instructor who saw a gap in students' scholarly writing or the adjunct who was challenged by the time involved with providing feedback. The American College of Education continually changes internal and external policies and practices to accommodate innovation. A vision from faculty, staff, or students can promote innovation. Wendelken, Danzinger, Rau, and Moeslein (2014) argue that a leader should set up a process in which everyone in the organization has an opportunity to participate in the development of organizational vision. A learning culture within the doctoral department and the college leads to innovative ideas and opportunities for supporting teaching and learning.

Transformation leaders are change agents who embrace the concept of mistakes and risks. When mistakes occur, there could be negative consequences for employees. Leadership within the American College of Education understands that if there are no mistakes, no one is taking risks (Spector, 2013). Staff and faculty should be willing to take risks knowing the mission and vision of an organization support creativity. Wonderful designs emerge from what could be perceived as failure. Developing a creative and innovative culture takes time, but starts with changing the lightbulb and maintaining transparency with staff, faculty, and students.

Listening can be a great learning opportunity. Ideas were presented to various levels of leadership, prior to the discussion of the writing course and exploring opportunities for providing faster feedback. Different leaders gave reasons why certain suggestions would not work, ranging from functionality in the LMS, scalability, or capacity. Ultimately, leaders listened to the faculty and student concerns and offered thoughts to improve the support for student writing, or provided alternative suggestions for consideration. Original ideas were revised. While some leaders may not relish having failed to listen, these experiences can be beneficial in assessing situations. Listening can lead to implementing changes or learning from experiences to build on the original idea.

Empowerment

Empowering faculty and staff to be creative and innovative provides opportunities for intellectual stimulation. Intellectual stimulation is a key part of leadership and problem solving. Zhou, Hirst, and Shipton (2012) found that leaders who intellectually stimulate others encourage creativity, accept challenges as part of the job, and solve problems in a rational manner. Transformational leaders develop other leaders through modeling. It is important for administration to share problem-solving techniques with faculty and staff to maintain student support in the absence of administration. Empowering future leaders to manage future projects increases and raises problem-solving skills in all environments.

A department chair needs support faculty and staff. Tasks and initiatives that are shared will balance responsibilities and create opportunities for professional growth. A benefit in sharing responsibilities is empowering others and creating leadership roles. Faculty sometimes need encouragement or prompting to take the initiative on projects. Wendelken et al. (2014) suggested employee initiative can result in career opportunities. The advantage for leadership and faculty is in appreciating the benefits of career opportunities and professional growth, in shared responsibilities.

Social Cognitive Learning Theory in Action

The social cognitive learning theory helps others feel more connected to a new concept as well as feel safe to try new strategies and take risks (Lemberger, Brigman, Webb, & Moore, 2012). Behavior, cognition, and social environment have a role in how and what is learned. The social learning theory embraces the idea of individuals learning in a variety of ways within a social environment: through direct experience, through indirect experience (by watching or observing others), and by storing and processing information. Through direct experience, faculty will provide the feedback, realize the benefits, embrace the challenge, and continue with the change initiative.

There are multiple opportunities for indirect learning experiences such as observation. Instructors can observe the leadership and repeat appropriate action, resulting in imitation. Leaders lead by example for this reason. Processing information through observation is a pathway in which some faculty will learn. To support the college and department initiative, faculty and staff will be coached and shown what specific feedback is required. Acquisition of feedback information can also occur through professional development and training. These opportunities will be discussed and implemented.

Consideration of the social learning theory is important in an organization when managing and leading others. During change transitions such as in a process or policy the benefits of the theory can be used to support smooth transitions. The department chair could lead discussions and demonstrate how others may gain indirect experience. Direct experiences are, also, vital in faculty training and acquisition of new knowledge to impacting and support change.

Reflections

When faculty look for change agents, the characteristics will include motivation and commitment. This motivation and commitment to making change and raising the quality of life for some conjure up technical leaders such as Steve Jobs. The determination of Steve Jobs led to a successful start-up, financial wealth, and life-changing (even societal) products (Finkle & Mallin, 2010). Skills alone do not lead to one being a change agent. One should remain optimistic when facing failures or moments of not having a clear solution. Through determination, the innovative spirit comes alive and helps to make other lives better.

Successes included the development of the writing course and overcoming faculty fears. Obstacles included the resistance to change from faculty. The development of the writing course emerged through the observation of student needs and courageous, yet collegiate discussions from faculty. Achievement of student success in writing is dependent on faculty participation. Some faculty are on point and some faculty are status quo. Several conversations and meetings took place to improve the program and fill the student writing gap. We offered more standardization for the teaching and learning, while leaving room for faculty to leave their fingerprint for academic freedom. The American College of Education doctoral students are supported to identify a problem or project, build their scholarship, and develop a dissertation to contribute to the literature in their field of study. We want our doctoral students to become solution creators and producers of knowledge.

CONCLUSION

Identifying processes to support all stakeholders within the teaching and learning environment involves multiple layers of communication. Consistent review of student needs and faculty needs is relevant to providing quality education. Developing a model to support stakeholders through the change process is a proactive approach. Implementing new knowledge from lessons learned and integration of evidence-based practices and theories for an effective change process will lead to resources for the constant cycle of change.

Interviews

"Light bulb moments" are often seen as being serendipitous and fleeting. I hope that the following interview questions and answers deepen understanding about how these moments can be cultivated and sustained. The "Light Bulb Moment Worksheet" (appendix) offers a framework for stimulating transformation at your college or university.

Changing the Light Bulb

David: How many academics does it take to change a light bulb?

Crystal: I have to laugh; that's a good question.

Imani: My collaborative mindset immediately says "you know, that's the way we work, we're a team." So all of us have some input in how to change the light bulb.

Crystal: I would have said at least three because one is going to start the discussion, the other person is going to add to it, and the other person is going to offer some kind of contrasting view on how it should be done. So it's going to take at least three. One person can definitely make a change, I just automatically start to think about a slight resistance or the question of "why?"

Imani: I do consider myself a change agent and I do know that if you want to stay current and as on top of it as possible, then you make it a point to bring in diversity or try to gain an outside perspective.

Question for Reader Reflection

How could differing views be included as a valuable part of transformative change at your institution?

Change Agency

David: How has your life prepared you to be a change agent?

Crystal: So what prepared me to be a change agent is the whole process of being flexible. I moved out of the country for a couple of years to Germany and it was literally a culture shock . . . you can map out all the things that could possibly go right or wrong but you're never going to really know until that actually happens. So for me I think having lived abroad helped me become a change agent in terms of the flexibility piece, but otherwise I think from a young child I always wanted to make a difference, though I didn't realize at the time that change was a part of it. Making a positive impact sometimes does require some changes.

Imani: When I look back on the trajectory of my life, when I reflect on talking to educators about the issue of poverty and resilience, I think about my life as a young child and how I was really in that category of being poor. I was considered at risk and I know I didn't like that so I would always make an effort to find opportunities.

And so . . . when I decided to teach I knew I wanted to work with students who were considered at risk or marginalized. I wanted to work with students who received specialized services. And in that role I had to be an advocate for my students, I had to work to make the people that I worked with, or who serviced these students, see these students in a different light instead of helpless. That our job was to elevate them to the next level because sometimes that mindset of Special Education is, you know, you enter a year or two there at one grade [level] and you remain there. I had to work with teachers, general education teachers, to open their minds up for inclusion and then that carried me to becoming a change agent. In this leadership role I found myself having a lack of resources. So my guiding thoughts were always "How can we do this this way?"

or "How can we make things better this way?" These guiding questions resulted in new ways of doing things. That's kind of how I see life prepared me to be the change agent that I am.

Crystal: I had to shake my head a lot when Imani spoke because I think the perspective of being at risk [is] why she and I get along so well, that we have a lot of similar viewpoints, because I think that at risk piece really has a lot to do with both of our backgrounds and I think that that's definitely where it comes in. Maybe you're not born to be a change agent, but I think that growing up at risk definitely kind of prepares you to do that.

Question for Reader Reflection

How have the challenges and opportunities that you faced in life prepared you to be a change agent?

Advice

David: What advice do you have for others who want to transform higher education?

Crystal: Try to get a coalition together . . . so they don't overwhelm themselves or get burned out. Having a right hand man or woman is very essential.

Imani: Just waiting for that right time. . . . She[Crystal] carries a heavy load, so if I'm talking to her and she's not totally listening to me, I know to come back to her at another time because she might be dealing with another issue. So just being able to manage your manager; that persistence piece, [that] emotional intelligence piece.

Question for Reader Reflection

How could you and your supervisor improve your ability to collaborate in support of desired outcomes?

REFERENCES

ACE (2017, January.). Student handbook, Version 10. *American College of Education*. Retrieved from https://www.ace.edu/docs/default-source/default-document-library/ace-student-handbook.pdf

American College of Education. (2016, November). 2016 annual assessment report: Overall and program-student learning outcomes results and conclusions. Retrieved from ace.edu

Badenhorst, C., Moloney, C., Rosales, J., Dyer, J., & Ru, L. (2015). Beyond deficit: Graduate student research-writing pedagogies. *Teaching in Higher Education, 20*(1), 1–11. doi:10.1080/13562517.2014.945160

Cotterall, S. (2011). Doctoral student's writing: Where's the pedagogy? *Teaching in Higher Education, 16*(4), 413–425. doi:10.1080/13562517.2011.560381

Dickens, L., & Watkins, K. (1999). Action research: Rethinking Lewin, *Management Learning, 30*(2). doi: /abs/10.1177/1350507699302002

Di Fabio, A., Bernaud, J., & Loarer, E. (2014). Emotional intelligence or personality in resistance to change? Empirical results in an Italian health care context. *Journal of Employment Counseling, 51*(4), 146–157. doi:10.1002/j.2161–1920.2014.00048.x

Finkle, T., & Mallin, M. L. (2010). Steve Jobs and Apple Inc. *Journal of the International Academy for Case Studies, 16*(8), 49–57. Retrieved from http://www.world cat.org/title/journal-of-the-international-academy-for-case studies/oclc/45405080

Frank, J. (2011). Let's huddle. *Medical Economics, 88*(5), 65–72. Retrieved from http://medicaleconomics.modernmedicine.com/

Gardner, H. (2006). *Changing minds: The art and science of changing our own and other people's minds.* Boston, MA: Harvard Business School Publishing.

Kulkarni, V. (2016). Employee interpretations of change: Exploring the other side of the resistance story. *Indian Journal of Industrial Relations, 52*(2), 246–263. Retrieved from http://www.publishingindia.com/ijir/

Lemberger, M. E., Brigman, G., Webb, L., & Moore, M. M. (2012). Student success skills: An evidence-based cognitive and social change theory for student achievement. *Journal of Education, 192*(2–3), 89–99. Retrieved from http://www.bu.edu/journalofeducation/

Lillis, T., & Turner, J. (2001). Student writing in higher education: Contemporary confusion traditional concerns. *Teaching in Higher Education, 6*(1), 57–68. doi:10.1080/13562510020029608

Scott, S. W., & Garland, G. (2007). Where to bury the survivors? Exploring possible ex post effect of resistance to change. *SAM Advanced Management Journal, 72*(1), 52–62. Retrieved from http://samnational.org/publications/sam-advanced-management-journal/

Spector, B. (2013). *Implementing organizational change: Theory into practice* (3rd ed.). Upper Saddle River, NJ: Pearson.

Wendelken, A., Danzinger, F., Rau, C., & Moeslein, K. M. (2014). Innovation without me: Why employees do (not) participate in organizational innovation communities. *R&D Management, 44*(2), 217–236. doi:10.1111/radm.12042

Zhou, Q., Hirst, G., & Shipton, H. (2012). Context matters: Combined influence of participation and intellectual stimulation on the promotion focus-employee creativity relationship. *Journal of Organizational Behavior, 33*(7), 894–909. doi:10.1002/job.779

Chapter 4

Catalyzed Change to Encourage Student Persistence in STEM

Dr. Nancy Kaufmann, Dr. Sarah Grubb,
and Dr. Marcie Warner

University of Pittsburgh, Pennsylvania

How many academics does it take to change a light bulb?

Top-Down and Bottom-Up Contributors

In this chapter, Dr. Nancy Kaufmann (assistant director of Undergraduate Research), Dr. Sarah Grubb (visiting laboratory instructor), and Dr. Marcie Warner (laboratory instructor) from the University of Pittsburgh, Department of Biological Sciences, share their work in the area of encouraging student persistence in STEM. During the interview, Nancy shared about how the work of her team is now part of an expanding momentum for innovation at the university:

> *Because we were making these huge changes our department—it got recognized at a higher level in the university—[and] I was able to meet people from other departments that are also trying to innovate in their department, which never happened before. I've been in this job for 10 years on multiple grants, but now our vice provost really brought people [together] to get innovative, people from different departments or people making innovations from different departments.*

INTRODUCTION

The current numbers of American graduates in science, technology, engineering, and mathematics (STEM) fields are insufficient to meet the predicted needs for skilled workers in these disciplines. Evidence continues to mount that offering authentic research experiences to students with an interest in

59

STEM fields during their early undergraduate experiences can increase graduation rates in these fields. With the support of the University and a grant from the Howard Hughes Medical Institute, we were able to design and implement a suite of research-based introductory biology laboratory courses based upon the research of our faculty in the Department of Biological Sciences at the University of Pittsburgh. We have successfully built an instructional team, built supportive relationships with research faculty, scaled the courses to meet the needs of a growing student population, and shared our experiences with the larger University community. We continue to refine our approaches to recruiting and training skilled faculty and undergraduate teaching assistants, continually updating curriculum to keep the research projects current, and helping students to find research opportunities after completing the course.

BACKGROUND AND CHALLENGES

It is well-established that too few American students currently enter and persist in the science and engineering fields. Attrition that begins in grade school continues through the university years where many college students who planned careers in science, engineering, and medicine leave STEM fields for humanities or leave college entirely. A 2012 report delivered to President Barack Obama (PCAST report Engage to Excel: Producing One Million Additional College Graduates with Degrees in Science, Technology, Engineering, and Mathematics) reported a need for an additional one million more STEM-trained workers by 2022. They pointed to the failure of many STEM-aspiring undergraduates to stay in STEM and suggested that increasing the persistence of STEM-aspiring undergraduates from 40 percent to 50 percent could account for the one million additional STEM graduates needed to support the U.S. economy.

The call to increase persistence was a radical idea at many large universities where introductory science courses often had a reputation as "weed-out" courses. Anecdotally, though many faculty wanted students to succeed in their courses, it was not unusual to hear faculty and students accepting the idea that some students "aren't cut out for being a doctor or a scientist." There was some thought that it might be a service provided to the community-at-large that students who were not succeeding in the courses left the field. As the Engage to Excel PCAST report was discussed in faculty and administrative meetings across the country, a transformation in attitude about the role of the introductory STEM courses and their instructors began to change. More scientists were now needed, not fewer. Faculty started thinking about how to change and supplement their courses to build more success among their students.

At the same time that PCAST called upon faculty to support more student persistence, faculty were already working through a set of two other reports that challenged them to transform their methods of teaching and assessing. There was growing concern among scientific and medical agencies that undergraduate science education was not properly training students with the skills they would need to be modern scientists or even science-aware citizens. Scientific Foundations for Future Physicians (AAMC and HHMI, 2009) and Vision and Change in undergraduate biology education: a call to action (AAAS, 2009) criticized the content-driven teaching of many science courses and challenged that STEM students were leaving college with heads full of facts but without knowing how to access new findings, interpret data of new findings, or even design experiments to generate new findings. In a time of fast scientific developments and generation of Big Data, these agencies called on universities to transform STEM education. The reports outlined specific competencies that undergraduate science programs, especially in biology, should now teach students.

Making the transformation from content-based to competency-based teaching presented many challenges for large universities. Introductory science courses were typically high-enrollment courses with limited resources or systems for development. While laboratories that accompanied these courses were often much smaller sections, historically they had typically presented hands-on demonstrations coupled tightly to lecture material. Instead of learning to think like scientists, students were memorizing facts and performing cookbook-like labs. In tight economic times for universities, it was hard to imagine how to move away from these efficient, inexpensive courses. The 2009 reports had, however, encouraged instructors to start developing inexpensive approaches to transformation and ways to encourage student thinking over memorization. The PCAST report followed through with specific recommendations for transformation.

The PCAST report called for the use of evidence-based teaching methods, including, but not limited to, specifically asking for movement away from traditional cookbook labs to "discovery-based" laboratory courses. They asked for diversification of teaching modalities, likely away from straight lecture and multiple choice exams; many recent papers had shown evidence that active methods better supported student learning (Armbruster, Patel, Johnson, & Weiss, 2009; Freeman et al., 2014). They also proposed creation of multiple paths for students to enter STEM.

Our Own Transformation Begins

Faculty in the Department of Biological Sciences at the University of Pittsburgh took notice of these reports and advances in teaching practices. Our student attrition statistics were in line with the national average and the diversity of our student body was well below the rest of the University. We began to encourage faculty to familiarize themselves with active learning techniques and to integrate them into their classes. At the same time, we began a small-scale introduction of discovery-based laboratory courses for early career students. These initial changes were positive and well-received by students and faculty. The Department was eager to expand these offerings, but scaling up these types of changes is typically slow; faculty must divert their energies from their current duties to learn new methods and develop new curriculum. It was good fortune that a major granting agency in the sciences, the Howard Hughes Medical Institute (HHMI), put out a call for proposals to support the very programs we were interested in expanding.

CHANGE INITIATIVE AND PLAN FOR CHANGE

In early 2013, the HHMI announced a call for five-year grant proposals to 203 research universities in "Sustaining Excellence: New awards for science education to research universities." They asked universities to tackle the problem of low persistence rates in STEM, focusing on the first two "early career" years of college where the biggest drop in STEM retention was seen. HHMI specifically cited the PCAST report and individual recommendations therein, including suggesting grant proposals should include a plan to replace traditional laboratory courses with discovery-based labs. Immediately, research universities across the nation began to develop plans for competition, knowing that only about thirty-five schools could expect to actually receive funding of approximately 2.5 million dollars each over five years.

The call by HHMI was an ingenious step toward driving nationwide change at research universities. Though many universities would not be funded, most invited schools would begin a plan and enter the competition. In order to enter, a university had to have letters of support from top administrators and financial support from the university. Thus, HHMI assured that across the country, colleges knew about the PCAST report and were thinking about addressing it. Another smart inclusion in the HHMI grant call was a demand that competitive proposals include a plan for sustainability beyond the coverage of the grant, and in year four of the grant, funded programs would have to demonstrate a developed plan for sustaining their transformation. Thus it was clear that the money was a stimulus, not renewable, and HHMI would promote change only if a university believed it could truly transform without further grant funding.

In the Department of Biological Sciences at the University of Pittsburgh, one of 115 large "R1" high-research-activity universities in the United States, we had already begun to discuss the above reports and make small changes to our introductory biology program when the grant call from HHMI came in. Slow and small changes, hard to build at a large institution, were now incentivized onto a fast time frame and at a large scale. We were especially attracted to the call for laboratory course transformation because we had already initiated change in that format. In our two-semester introductory biology series, we had a single section of a two-semester research lab, SEA-PHAGES, in which students discovered and characterized viruses that infect bacteria. This course was part of a national program funded by HHMI and based on research from a faculty member's lab. We also had a second-semester introductory biology lab course based on research of water channel proteins from another lab in the department, begun with previous funding from HHMI. A course in novel antibiotic discovery was also developing as part of the national Small World Initiative program. We decided to design a grant proposal around the expansion of sections for courses already started and the development of new courses anchored in the research of faculty in the Department of Biological Sciences where the grant would be housed and administrated, if funded.

Many freshmen who enter introductory biology plan a biology major or came to an "R1" university because they want to do research, but the introductory curriculum is usually too time intensive for them to begin in a faculty lab. They also typically do not come to college with lab skills, nor do they know how to contact faculty to get involved in research. By designing introductory lab courses around faculty research active in the Department of Biological Sciences, we reasoned that we could support student retention through connecting them to real faculty research in the department. Because their work would contribute to faculty research in the department, there would be real meaning attributed to their work and this was expected to provide motivation noted as lacking in the PCAST report. Additionally, students would learn lab skills relevant to the faculty and faculty labs in the department could benefit from the contributions of hundreds of researchers in introductory labs. We had to pick from among approximately thirty faculty labs in the department, and design syllabi that could realistically work on a fourteen-week plan and produce meaningful results for students to analyze and faculty to use. Recalling the PCAST challenge to diversify pathways to enter STEM, we also wanted our courses to represent the diversity from ecology and evolution to molecular biology in the department.

While this was a daunting task, especially under the grant proposal timetable, we used "seven attributes for designing successful undergraduate research projects," developed from experiences in developing the virus hunting program (Hatfull et al., 2006). As we began to think about research in the department to include in the proposal, we used these seven attributes to guide our choice, starting with the need for the research to be real and publishable, contributing new knowledge that the scientific community would care about. Each student would have to know that their contributions were meaningful and thus establish some ownership over their part of the project (e.g., discovery of a new virus, crosses with a unique mutant, studying a spider they had captured). Thus students in each course would all work in parallel, each with a small difference that made their work meaningful and different from that of their neighbor or neighboring team.

In addition to the need for technical and conceptual simplicity of the projects, we looked for projects that could work on a once-a-week, three-hour lab schedule that the traditional courses already observed. It was essential that the faculty from whose research the course was generated believe that the data and materials generated by the students would be useful to their research and they had a support structure in their lab that would receive and build upon the work done by the students. The expectation was that the courses for transformation would produce publishable data and reagents. If not, the work would not be considered authentic and would certainly not be part of a sustainable plan. We had five courses in mind that represented the department diversity of research and appeared to be compatible with an introductory biology course level.

Once we had identified faculty research projects that fit these parameters, we developed fourteen-week syllabi for each course, taking direction from the AAAS and HHMI/AAMC competency-based plans (AAAS, 2009; AAMC and HHMI, 2009). It was essential that students be able to participate in all parts of the scientific method, not just tool developers or data collectors. They needed to evaluate the data they collected. Repetition of experiments was essential for being able to analyze data as a scientist, but this was an extreme departure from the survey one-week per project pattern of traditional labs. We had to leave the mindset that introductory labs were a place to expose students to myriad techniques and instead think of the student as scientist where some repetition would build feelings of expertise that might be important for persistence. For example, students utilize the technique of serial dilutions in several different contexts in SEA-PHAGES; they first utilize the technique to visualize the characteristics of their virus when grown on solid media and then to calculate the concentration of viral particles in liquid solution. Wary of student boredom that might drop motivation, we built in a few different techniques in each course and since real research often fails, we looked for places where there could be achievement "milestones" on the way to more complex experiments (Hatfull et al., 2006). These milestones can include visualizing a cell or virus utilizing microscopy or measuring concentrations of recovered DNA in a spectrophotometer or agarose gel.

Our proposal was to replace the traditional biology 2 lab course with a set of five choices of research authentic courses. We felt equipped only to focus on one semester of lab and already had initiated more transition at the biology 2 level. We reasoned the students in biology 1 lab would gain skills that would help them in the research courses. Additionally, the biology 1 lab was already well into a discovery-based transition. Though not real research, students in biology 1 were already designing experiments to test their own hypotheses and writing small research proposals. The biology 2 lab at that time was primarily survey and more cookbook style. The plan was designed to be sustainable since it swapped old courses for new. Evidence that research lab course "stream" structure promotes STEM retention has recently been published using a model at the University of Texas, Austin, campus (Rodenbusch, Hernandez, Simmons, & Dolan, 2016).

Our ability to actually run the courses demanded that we get the grant funding in line with a sustainability plan. We put together a budget, trying to anticipate costs of personnel, equipment, and supplies. Students in labs often pay lab fees, but the lab fees had remained stagnant for years and were very low. They would not cover the consumable supplies students would use in these new courses, so we put in a proposal to slowly raise lab fees in all biology laboratory courses, cognizant of the price of a typical biology textbook in a nonlab course. To initiate the courses, we would need new equipment specific for the different types of research projects, and sought grant funds to cover these one-time costs. The bulk of the financial request in the grant was to cover personnel who would develop and lead the courses. Section instructors would be funded primarily by the department because instructors that had been teaching the traditional lab course, funded by the department, could transition to teaching the new authentic research courses as they replaced sections of the traditional lab. Research faculty on whose work the course was based could help teach in the courses as part of their teaching responsibility.

Accompanying the grant proposal were letters of support from different high-level administrative areas of the University. Some letters pledged funds to parts of the budget, including costs of equipment, personnel, and summer fellowship funds for undergraduates from the courses to continue their research outside of the grant or travel to national meetings to present their research. These letters were an essential part of the package, as understood by HHMI. Large, sustainable transformation would need support from the top as well as the grass roots. The letters showed HHMI that administrators across the university were on board. We submitted the proposal and began to wait.

SUCCESSES AND OBSTACLES

In mid-2014 we were excited to hear that our proposal for transformation was accepted. The University of Pittsburgh was one of thirty-seven institutions that were funded and one of nine with a focus on introductory lab transformation. Grant awards are often accompanied by a cut in funding, and our grant was no exception. We had to quickly rebudget for the lower level of funding and then get to work to have a team in place when the grant started. Grant-catalyzed transformation happens fast on the grant's time frame and it does not slow down. We needed to be ready.

A Transformation Team

We searched for two research educators to join the grant team. They would be essential for the success of the transformation as they would provide the bridge for research from the five faculty principal investigator (PI) labs to the students and other section instructors. These research educators would need to interpret the science of the PI and develop curricula that students could actually do by transforming and writing protocols for each week of each course. They would need to have a deep understanding of the level of the students in the course to provide materials that truly supported student understanding of the research.

We had initially planned to hire one prep staff and one research educator but had two strong research educator applicants and made the smart decision to hire them both. The research educators that we hired each had a PhD in biology but had developed additional postdoctoral experience focused on science education. That their PhDs were from our department was an added benefit, as they were already deeply familiar with much of the research in the department as well as most of the PI's on the project. Additionally, they had each already designed and taught a biology 2 level research lab course. In retrospect, we may not have been able to offer the diversity of research course choices without both of them. While we proposed specific research PI labs for the grant, one of the research educators brought an additional PI connection to the team, with a course that she had already developed and piloted. This course actually may be the most adaptable to large-scale implementation of the set.

Course Launch and Expansion

Coming into the transition team with experience and expertise, the two research educators quickly began to teach in the preexisting research lab courses, expanding the number of sections of these courses in the first year. Teaching in these courses allowed them to begin to identify strengths and weaknesses of the framework for research course design to apply to the new courses they were developing. Within the first grant-funded year they had expanded our program from four to fifteen sections of biology 2 lab courses.

By the end of the second year the program had developed and launched three new research lab courses. Approximately 40 percent of the students in a biology 2 lab by the end of the second year of the grant were in an authentic research experience. By year three, the instructional team in charge of the traditional lab had transformed their biology 2 lab as well. While cost of the courses was a concern of many administrators, all newly developed lab courses have supply costs the same or less than upper division labs and come in or under the price of a biology textbook. Many of the courses shared equipment with each other or with upper division labs, and thus these aspects of the program seem very sustainable in the absence of grant funding. Excitingly, and unexpectedly the traditional lab group was inspired to develop their own addition to the research lab course suite. Faster than we anticipated, every biology 2 student was participating in the science of discovery.

The changing nature of authentic research presents the unique challenge that we will frequently need to update the research in the courses to keep the research relevant to the faculty labs. Because the quality of the student data and record keeping can be variable from these emerging scientists, we have built in more trial repetition across sections or terms in collecting data. For instance, where a typical biologist might do an experiment three times, we might have six or nine trials in the course setting. Thus the time frame is slower in our setting. We have tried to anticipate this in picking projects with the research faculty member, hoping to avoid being scooped by outsiders or the lab itself. We think the projects the students will do will produce interesting, meaningful results but are not in areas of heavy competition and are the types of experiments that can benefit from the parallel project input from students.

We have also tried to build in avenues for easy upgrades in working on the initial research design with the faculty. The SEA-PHAGES program has infinite room for discovery of new viruses, simply based on the estimate of how many unique bacteriophage are on the planet. Additionally, students in the course are now hunting for viruses that infect a different bacterial host than the course started with. In a course using spiders, research could move to a different species of local spider or other arthropod's behavior and microbiome. In a course using *Drosophila* genetics, students will move from searching for interacting genes on the second chromosome to a different chromosome and then move to other genes of interest in the lab. While the "Water Channels" course currently studies the stability of aquaporin water channel mutants, other human disease proteins can easily be studied in this model system using the same assays. Thus, we expect student findings in the courses to be relevant to the research faculty labs for years to come.

Are the courses producing useful data for the research faculty labs? While faculty labs have established differing levels of connection with the course, all have built upon results from the courses. Papers are regularly published with research from the SEA-PHAGES program and other courses are contributing to papers in the pipeline.

Developing the Instructor Teams

Transformation on this scale demanded the training of new course section instructors. By year three of the grant, fifteen people had trained to instruct in the research biology labs; however, some of those were graduate students or part-time workers who moved on to other positions. Others were the research educators, the faculty researcher of one course, and many were part-time instructors; thus most instructors had a limited amount of time to dedicate to teaching multiple sections of the courses. The difficulties and advantages of working in the framework of a large adjunct teaching program is well-known in academia and certainly not unique to our biology program, but the research lab course curriculum added to these challenges.

In training instructors, we needed to give them the information to understand the background and significance of the research. They also needed to learn how to use the equipment and do the experiments that the students would do. For many of them, the research area and type of experiments were new to them. Sometimes the experiments that the students would do were still being optimized because we had to launch the courses on a tight timescale, such that the students had a role in developing the methods of the research. With multiple research courses running each term, there needed to be a separate training plan for each course. We found it most effective to schedule the new instructor's sections later in the week than continuing instructors so that the new instructor could see the week's work in action and then adjust to fit their teaching style. Team-teaching between research faculty and research educators also exposed the research faculty to evidence-based teaching strategies and the research educators to a deep understanding of the research project.

In addition to the challenges of learning the specific science for each research project, the approach to teaching open-ended, authentic research was new to many instructors. They would need to transmit the meaningfulness of each student's results and analysis. Students were used to instructors knowing the answers to questions, but now the answers were truly unknown. This could be frustrating to some students or simply surprising. New instructors would be helping each student develop ownership of his or her own part in the parallel research projects. Students would be learning lab skills in the context of the real data they were collecting and would have to exercise care in performing procedures correctly for the data to be useful. The format of student evaluation was also different in the authentic research labs, as assignments involved preparing for journal club and generating figures for a research poster symposium at the end of each term.

Though these challenges cannot be ignored, we found new instructors to be excited to participate in this new style of instruction. Many had received excellent training in inquiry-based instruction during the development of the biology 1 traditional labs, while others were training in evidence-based teaching as part of the national Center for the Integration of Teaching and Learning (CIRTL) learning community (https://www.cirtl.net/). Our new instructors were willing to put in many hours knowing that they were part of something new; however, as transformation leaders we continue to try to balance the workload on the instructor appropriately and to get their feedback on how to improve training. (As we write this, the Department has just begun accepting applications for two new full-time instructor positions and we are optimistic that others will follow.)

Part of our instructional plan was to include undergraduate teaching assistants in the new lab courses. We reasoned that students who had already taken the course would be inspiring near-peer mentors for the students in the course, which should help encourage persistence. Undergraduate Teaching Assistant (UTAs) could provide additional skill instruction for students as many techniques would be new and challenging to students. Some UTAs might have more experience with a technique than novice instructors and thus provide support for them. Additionally, a UTA program provided a stream for students from the courses to continue a connection with the research, helping with the challenge of the limited number of independent undergraduate research positions in the PI labs.

We have implemented two to three UTAs in every authentic research lab section while we continue to develop best practices in training them in the challenge of near-peer instruction. Setting UTA training times is particularly challenging for research educators working around the UTAs' busy schedules. For individual instructors, the benefits of the UTAs bring with it the concealed challenge of more students in the room to organize and manage, often without feeling they have the authority to dismiss a distracting UTA. The department as a whole has seen a rapid growth in inclusion of UTAs in lecture and lab courses and we anticipate that this will lead to coming guidelines in their training and evaluation.

National Transformation Impact

In three years, faculty, graduate students, postdocs, and undergraduates who have participated in this transformative process in undergraduate education number in the hundreds, just within our Department of Biological Sciences. As the students, postdocs, and part-time instructors go to teach or research in other places, they will take with them the understanding that beginning undergraduates can all do real research and that the lab classroom is an ideal setting for a first experience in research.

Diversifying Pathways to STEM

The PCAST report called upon universities to open new avenues for STEM entry by students. As such, the University of Pittsburgh began looking more closely at the traditional path taken by introductory biology students. Most freshmen took introductory chemistry with a chemistry lab, introductory biology, and the introductory biology lab, sometimes with the addition of calculus, all within the first semester in college. In fact, this was not an atypical trajectory in life sciences programs across the country, but biology instructors and administrators at the University of Pittsburgh hypothesized that it might be part of the problem with STEM retention. Students identified by advisors as "at risk" were often suggested to spread out this course set. After examining the data, the biology department decided to encourage this for most incoming students, putting together a proposal to make the biology 1 lecture course a prerequisite for the biology 1 lab and biology 2 lecture would become a prerequisite for biology 2 lab.

For the new research lab biology 2 courses, this meant that most students would now take biology 2 lab in the first semester of their sophomore year, having a whole year and a summer to mature, acclimate to college, and begin to focus their interests. The proposal dovetailed with our development of a suite of research lab choices directed at different specialty areas within our department's biology program. Students deeper in to their science training would have more science experiences that would help direct their choice. With choice should come agency in their educational plan and higher likelihood of student persistence, we hoped.

The SEA-PHAGES research lab program stayed outside of this prerequisite requirement, allowing first semester freshmen to begin the virus hunting course while taking the biology lecture course. Thus students who had a strong research interest would be able to foster their growth as scientists from the beginning, which we hoped would help keep high-achieving students in biology even if they found the lecture course unengaging. Students identified as "at risk" by their advisors might also be prompted to take SEA-PHAGES in their first semester while putting off biology 1 lecture until the second semester. They would get the benefit of a small class setting mixed with the excitement of being part of a national virus discovery team of undergraduates and be less likely to feel "behind" in their science course sequences having already completed a lab when many of their peers had not. Having built new pathways to enter and stay in the biology program, we have responded to the PCAST call and expect more of our students to successfully stay in STEM. While some might see the prerequisite of lecture for lab as an obstacle for most students to get to the exciting authentic research labs, we believe that for most students, the informed choice in their sophomore year will lead to better outcomes and for others the SEA-PHAGES program offers an impressive alternative.

Developments Elsewhere in the University

Throughout the University, there have been a number of successes of programs in the STEM field that have helped our program. The University of Pittsburgh established a center (dB-SERC) where science instructors share innovations and discuss and develop evidenced-based teaching methods. The center encourages course developments with small grants, of which our SEA-PHAGES course was a beneficiary, and has begun a UTA training workshop. Graduate students, postdoctoral scholars, and even faculty are receiving explicit instruction in evidence-based teaching practices through a national certification program called the CIRTL in which the University of Pittsburgh is one of forty-three universities participating (https://www.cirtl.net/). CIRTL trainees have sought out teaching opportunities in our authentic research courses. In addition to these two education centers on campus, there have been developments within individual departments within the university. The chemistry department developed a new research-based organic chemistry lab option that is a continuation of the Small World biology research lab.

Other Obstacles

Because we had support from administrative groups at grant submission, and then received grant funding, we had broad university support, affording us the luxury of focusing on the internal challenges of course development and instructor training discussed earlier. We note some other obstacles that we did not anticipate.

The impact of the authentic research courses relies on the feeling of students and instructors that their work is meaningful. While there is no question that students are excited about these courses and value the new options available to them, there still seems to be a mindset from traditional education that creates a barrier. A couple of UTAs from different courses recently revealed misconceptions that specific experiments were done for "training" or because they were techniques "that all students should learn." Certainly the research educators consider student education while designing materials, but the experiments chosen are always ones for which the research labs want data to better understand their biological process of interest. If some UTAs, who have in fact worked in the research lab, have the mindset that some experiments are simply "exercises" then surely many students in the course believe this as well. More savvy students sometimes ask about the research that was done in the previous semester and what was learned. Students do not always appreciate the essentiality of repetition in science and may feel that they are simply "verifying" instead of making new discoveries. These are places where we need to work with instructors and UTAs to transparently share previous findings, produce publications, and work on the message of the specific relevance of each experiment to the research lab.

The large amount of material preparation in lab courses is not unique to the authentic research labs, but by offering a suite of different labs within a term, we increased the complexity of preparation substantially (crickets to feed spiders, vials of yeast media for fruit flies, plates of media for yeast, etc.). Meanwhile, the traditional lab team still needed to prepare materials for all of their courses which continued to run. In the grant proposal we planned to hire a person who would do all preparation and ordering for the new labs, but in hindsight that was too much for one person. When we interviewed people for the preparation job, we had no candidates that matched that level but instead had a couple of excellent candidates for the research educator position. By choosing to hire two research educators and no prep leader, we created the obstacle that the research educators would also be in charge of the preparation and ordering for their courses. While this gave them more confidence in the materials made than they might otherwise have had, it presented another level of work to their position. They now manage students who do the bulk of the preparation.

Sometimes faculty leave! A successful lab course lost its connection to research in the department when the faculty researcher moved to another institution across the country. In the short term, we need to be flexible and continue the research, using modern ways of communication to keep the research connection real. As a longer term goal, we are working to redesign this course so that it will continue to have connections to research being done within our department.

Students thoroughly enjoy doing research, but we have encountered difficulty with finding opportunities for students to be able to perform as much research as they would like. As potential solutions to this problem, we have added more open-lab hours outside of class time, while lab room space is already strained. We sometimes take on more UTAs than we need because students want to continue, though this means more people for us to train. We offer summer fellowships for students to continue research and sponsor them in research faculty labs outside the department. Still, we need to find more ways for students to continue their research. Toward this end, we have developed a curriculum vitae writing workshop and specifically encourage students to include their authentic course-based experiences. Every semester we hold a poster session in which all the students in the courses participate, to give them experience in writing and talking about their research. We also sponsor a poster session of students who are in faculty labs across the university and as a forum in which our course students can learn about opportunities outside their research faculty's lab. While "too much interest" in continuing research is a great problem for us to have, it continues to be a challenge for our department and our institution.

LESSONS LEARNED AND CONTINUED CHALLENGES

Grant proposals are excellent vehicles for catalyzing institutional change, and in this case answering a series of national calls for educational transformation. The pathway to transformation may be different from those specifically outlined in the grant and this is OK. People working on grant implementation may not anticipate where paths will differ, but must be flexible as long as the new plans fully support the spirit of the grant.

For instance, we were flexible from the very beginning of hiring our research educator team and designing the specific research projects for the lab courses. Our decision to hire two research educators instead of one research educator and one prep staff has provided us the opportunity to expand our course repertoire and allowed us to develop a course that can easily be scaled to run as many sections as we need to provide all students an authentic research experience within our department, which would not have been possible without the second research educator. We also did not anticipate losing a research faculty member connected to one of the research courses to a university across the country. The lesson we have taken from this is to always be looking for the next research lab and the next project to develop. The environment of academics suggests this can happen again when we least expect it. Already lessons from specific lab courses are helping us figure out what works well and what does not in these courses; we have become more facile at developing projects and can quickly build a syllabus once we have the project.

Students love research. They do not want to stop. Finding avenues that allow students to continue to be involved in research even after they have completed the courses is essential. We have worked hard to make this possible for our students by providing opportunities to become UTAs in the research-based labs, offering summer fellowships within labs in our department, and helping them match with other research labs outside of the department to learn new skills. We continue to search for additional opportunities to keep our students engaged and excited about research.

Our biggest lesson is to set limits for ourselves. Grant-initiated change is a strong catalyst of transformation, but the speed of the process presents challenges. We are learning not to overextend with the number of course choices we offer students in a semester and the amount of choice for projects within the syllabus. While we know student choice is important, we are looking into developing tools to assess how much choice is the right amount for them and the research educators and instructors. Communication with other teaching faculty and getting their input can also be sacrificed when making change quickly, but of course their connection to our curricular changes are important as we build this transformation into a sustained, critical piece of our undergraduate curriculum.

CONCLUSION

The transformation of our early career introductory biology labs was motivated by the desire to increase persistence in STEM at our university and transform teaching and assessment styles to be in line with the national PCAST, Scientific Foundations for Future Physicians, and Vision and Change initiatives; however, this transformation would not have been possible without the timely HHMI call for grant proposals. We have made great strides in the development of our program and we are looking forward to being able to assess how these changes have impacted our students as they continue in upper-level courses at the university and graduate and pursue their careers.

Interviews

"Light bulb moments" are often seen as being serendipitous and fleeting. I hope that the following interview questions and answers deepen understanding about how these moments can be cultivated and sustained. The "Light Bulb Moment Worksheet" (appendix) offers a framework for stimulating transformation at your college or university.

Changing the Light Bulb

David: How many academics does it take to change a light bulb?

Nancy: (Laughter) Well I think that what's important is that the academics are in different places in the academic system. It can't be [just] top down; can't be just bottom up. You need support in different places.

Marcie: I think we have departmental support here. Before we even got involved in bringing in these research-based courses that undercurrent to the department was to move towards active learning and incorporating new teaching methods that help to retain students in the sciences.

Question for Reader Reflection

How could your college/university improve its ability to provide multiple levels of support to leverage change initiatives?

Change Agency

David: How has your life prepared you to be a change agent?

Marcie: I do know that I've always tried to make sure I'm not one of those people who's afraid of change.

Nancy: We were first researchers and so we take a research approach to education. And so . . . if people are publishing evidence that research-based lab courses help students to stay in science, great. If there's research out there then we feel like we should pay attention to that and not ignore it, not be afraid of it. I think that having a research background was important.

Sarah: I come from a family of teachers, mainly elementary school teachers. Every family event is focused on them talking about education in some way. And so I thought a lot, not specifically just about science, but about teaching in lots of different levels and the way to get students motivated and interested.

Marcie: I didn't wake up one day and say, "Oh, I want to change things," but certainly I have had experiences that made me see the value of the way that we teach. So as an undergraduate I sat in lecture courses for three years or so and then one day I got to do a technique that I had heard about, you know, 10 times and all of a sudden it was just like, "Oh, that's how it works!" So giving the students opportunities to do that very early on in their career I think puts them in a better position to learn when they are in a lecture setting.

Sarah: I had some really fantastic female mentors and advisors in undergrad as both professors and research advisors and I've always wanted to be that same role model for the students. And I like the way we've designed our courses so that we have the opportunity to really interact with the students and get to know them and be role models and help them along their path.

Question for Reader Reflection

How does your professional background inform your approach to being an agent of change?

Advice

David: What advice do you have for others who want to transform higher education?

Nancy: I would say to find people at all different levels in your university that might be interested [in transformation] and get a cohort group that transcends different levels and different types. Find the people who are interested and get them together to try to find ways to support your initiative.

Question for Reader Reflection

Who could you enlist to be part of a cohort of support for the transformational initiative you envision?

REFERENCES

American Association for the Advancement of Science. (2009). *Vision and change in undergraduate biology education: A call to action*. Retrieved from http://vision andchange.org/finalreport/

Armbruster, P., Patel, M., Johnson, E., & Weiss, M. (2009). Active learning and student-centered pedagogy improve student attitudes and performance in introductory biology. *CBE Life Sciences Education, 8*(3), 203–213.

Association of American Medical Colleges and Howard Hughes Medical Institute. (2009). *Scientific foundations for future physicians*. Retrieved from https://www.aamc.org/download/271072/data/scientificfoundationsforfuturephysicians.pdf

Freeman, S., Eddy, S. L., McDonough, M., Smith M. K., Okoroafor, N., Jordt, H., & Wenderoth, M. P. (2014). Active learning increases student performance in science, engineering, and mathematics. *Proceedings of the National Academy of Science of the USA, 111*(23), 8410–8415.

Hatfull, G. F., Pedulla, M. L., Jacobs-Sera, D., Cichon, P. M., Foley, A., Ford, M. E., . . . & Hendrix, R. W. (2006). Exploring the mycobacteriophage metaproteome: Phage genomics as an educational platform. *PLoS Genetics, 2*(6), e92.

Rodenbusch, S. E., Hernandez, P. R., Simmons, S. L., & Dolan, E. L. (2016). Early engagement in course-based research increases graduation rates and completion of science, engineering, and mathematics degrees. *CBE Life Sciences Education, 15*(2), 1–10.

Chapter 5

Issues, Obstacles, and Challenges of Systematic Change in Curriculum and Instruction

Dr. Jennifer G. Beasley and Dr. Derrick Mears

University of Arkansas, Arkansas

How many academics does it take to change a light bulb?

An Elastic Number Based on the Scope of Work

In this chapter Dr. Jennifer Beasley (director of teacher education, Boyer Center for Student Service) and Dr. Derrick Mears (clinical associate professor and EdS program coordinator, Department of Curriculum & Instruction, CIED) share how they worked to generate systemic change in curriculum and instruction at the University of Arkansas. I was touched during the interview when they spoke about the catharsis and celebration that came from writing the chapter.

> Jennifer: *We have loved the opportunity [to write this chapter]. It's really helped us think about things from looking down, and looking at, our past. What we've done and what we need to change.*

> Derrick: *Thanks a lot thanks for the opportunity. I think it was kind of therapeutic for us to be able to sit down and say: "OK, wow, we have done some things." Because some days you feel like "we haven't gotten anywhere three years." And so that was what was great about writing this chapter; we realized, "gosh look at where we have come in a three year period."*

INTRODUCTION

How does a graduate program in higher education facilitate systemic change? This was our guiding question when we assumed the roles of Graduate Coordinator and Educational Specialist Coordinator in the Department of

Curriculum and Instruction at the University of Arkansas in 2014. Our programs were by no means floundering. We were ranked in the top 100 among schools of education by U.S. News and World Report and had active programs at the Master's, Educational Specialist, and Doctoral levels. However, we felt there were many ways we could improve. We hope this chapter serves as a case study for those who serve in similar roles at their universities. It merely describes our journey, which in some cases is typical while in others atypical. It also outlines our areas of success, as well as the challenges, initiatives, and obstacles we faced along the way.

BACKGROUND

The Department of Curriculum and Instruction is the largest department in the College of Education and Health Professions at the University of Arkansas. The department consists of twenty-seven full-time tenure-track faculty and nineteen clinical faculty that have a variety of roles in multiple programs. Our graduate programs consist of Master's degrees in Career and Technical Education, Childhood Education, Curriculum and Instruction, Educational Leadership, Educational Technology, Special Education, Secondary Education, and Teaching English to Second Language Learners. Also housed in the department are Educational Specialist and Doctoral programs in Curriculum and Instruction and Educational Leadership. A series of graduate certificates are also offered which provide specialized training/continuing education and/or additional licensure to practicing K–12 educators. During academic year 2017 the department provided coursework to over 350 graduate students not including students taking courses from outside of the department. Administratively in addition to a full-time department head, seven program coordinators manage the multiple degree programs and serve on a part-time basis in addition to their other duties as faculty members. There is also a part-time assistant department head who coordinates all graduate programs. The coordinators meet on a monthly basis to collaboratively manage programs in the department and the entire graduate faculty meets as a group on a monthly basis as well. The department also has twelve funded graduate assistants (GAs) that serve in a teaching and research capacity while pursuing doctoral study.

CHALLENGES

When we assumed the roles of Graduate Coordinator and Education Specialist Coordinator, we had the dual challenges of both learning our roles and understanding the changing landscape of our institution. Both of us had come from faculty teaching positions and were adding these new responsibilities, so assuming administrative roles required us to begin to gain an understanding of university advancement priorities. Our university was in a time of administrative transition. The chancellor would soon be stepping down to return to faculty, the provost was leaving to assume a similar role at another university, and our dean was also transitioning back to a faculty position within our department. Our first lesson learned was that change creates challenges. During this time of transformation the challenges in which we faced could be characterized into three categories, namely: (a) challenges related to conflicting demands of leadership, (b) challenges in balancing the needs of faculty with the needs of students, and (c) challenges in adapting to the era of accountability in higher education.

Conflicting Demands of Leadership

To serve in a leadership capacity in any organization an individual has to balance multiple demands. Literature on leadership in higher education seems to have either a *leader*-centric focus or a *community*-centric focus (Dopson et al., 2016). A substantial amount of research on leadership in higher education focuses on how a leader builds his or her skills to impact change. A smaller number of studies focus on how leadership for transformational change depends on working within a system. At our university it was important for us to understand our community and the system if we had any hope to facilitate change. Our department was part of larger college and university that was in the midst of flux. When thinking of the changes that needed to take place, we were faced with many unknowns about the future direction of the university, college, and/or department. In addition to not knowing who would be our future dean, provost, and chancellor, we balanced the conflicting demand of increasing the number of graduate students while increasing selectivity to improve national rankings. In the first semester of our new positions, we received a list of the average Graduate Record Examination (GRE) scores for our doctoral students as compared to other programs within our college. We were given direction by administration to tighten the admission standards and selectively admit students who had higher GRE scores. At the same time our graduate school was encouraging us to increase enrollment in our graduate degrees. Which should be the focus?

Balancing the Needs of Faculty with the Needs of Students

In any university, there are faculty members that are very committed to their content expertise and subsequently have courses that are tied to their research interests. In our department, we have faculty who have been teaching some courses for over ten years and they have a sense of ownership in that course. As new faculty come into the department with new ideas and interests in changing coursework or teaching new courses, this can become a type of territorial war between faculty members. Discussions about whether a course should continue to be offered to doctoral students can become a battleground during faculty meetings. Another key challenge was related to meeting the needs of our students. We needed to identify the key knowledge and skill sets that our graduates should possess to be quality practitioners in the various fields related to curriculum and instruction. With over 250 courses listed (10 percent were actually being taught on a regular basis), we had to take on the laborious challenge of examining what courses should make up our degree programs. With each course, we needed to develop a consistent course rotation that led students to obtain their degree in a timely manner while having sufficient enrollment in courses to make them financially viable. Also we sought to examine how we should deliver the content: whether in traditional sessions; seminars; synchronous online; asynchronous online in addition to whether we were matching faculty expertise to curriculum.

Adapting to the Era of Accountability

A third challenge was the new program accountability measures implemented at our university. As former K–12 practitioners we were both used to the idea of developing and implementing standardized assessments tied to learning outcomes, but for many of our programs being asked to collect, analyze, and articulate measures of student learning at the programmatic level was a new initiative. As part of this initiative we had to begin to look at how to effectively collect, analyze, and utilize resultant data to facilitate programmatic change. We considered this a positive thing and began to use this type of systematic evaluation system for many of our programs.

In addition to collecting program data, during our second year in our positions, we had the added challenge of having our EdS and PhD programs externally evaluated. In this level of accountability we would not only report to our department, but to our university as well.

CHANGE INITIATIVE

As Michael Fullan (2007) notes, "All successful change processes have a 'bias for action'" (p. 41). It was evident in our own department that there was a desire for action on the part of the faculty, students, and administration.

What remained unclear was what Hord and Roussin (2013) refer to as the "why," "what," and "how" of that change. To begin, we needed to articulate our shared goals, establish standards for our work, and create an invitation for collaboration.

Initial Steps: Initiation

From the beginning, the leadership together with the faculty established three goals for the graduate programs, (a) clarity, (b) transparency, and (c) identity. We began framing all meetings by using the language of these stated goals and organizing any efforts and decisions under those goals. In terms of clarity, it was important for the department to be clear about the goals as well as expectations for the graduate programs. The faculty initially listed goals such as developing a clear list of graduate courses, primarily for the doctoral program.

The second goal for the department was transparency. Decisions concerning the selection of GAs as well as student admission were at times unclear. Many faculty had articulated a desire to be aware of decisions and how they were made. We made each graduate faculty meeting agenda available the week before the meeting through a Google document so that they could add questions and issues that they wanted to discuss during the meeting.

Finally, the program was in need of identity. A few of our initial questions were: Who were our graduates? What careers were we preparing them for? Would we say we had an identity as a program? If we were to start recruiting for our graduate programs, what helped us to stand out above the rest?

In addition to having very clear goals as we initiated change, it was important to establish norms for collaboration. After the first few meetings, it was apparent that the faculty needed to cocreate process standards for working toward established goals. The faculty broke up into small groups and brainstormed norms for collaboration. After some discussion, the following norms were adopted:

1. Construct an environment where individuals engage in dialogue over issues, can ask for clarification, feel comfortable speaking the truth, and agree to disagree respectfully.
2. Identify the goals for each meeting and maintain a productive focus of interactive decision making.
3. Outline ideas and accomplishments and establish a schedule at the conclusion of each meeting.
4. Establish an environment where ideas are valued and considered.
5. Establish an environment of collegial civil discourse where faculty engage in positive interactions.

As this work began, we saw more collaboration and community-building on the part of the faculty. After the first couple of meetings, we added a component to every meeting called "Kudos" where we began the meeting by announcing any faculty accomplishments from published papers, to family events. Slowly, the community began to build and we were ready to implement some of our shared goals.

Beginning Work: Implementation

In the first six months, the faculty began working toward shared goals. During a change cycle, participants can experience a variety of emotions. Kelly and Conner (1979) describe this as an emotional change cycle. At the onset, participants tend to approach change with uninformed optimism (see figure 5.1). As we began our work together, there was evidence of this optimism.

A few tasks we tackled early on were selecting courses in our doctoral program and GA selection. By focusing on our identity and clarity of goals we began to cull through the myriad of courses listed in our graduate catalog. The faculty began by doing a sort activity with the course titles. We broke the groups up and gave one group all courses associated with curriculum and instruction, one group all courses concerning research, and finally one group looking at courses directed toward social justice and policy. The faculty was enthusiastic and they made short work of the task.

A second task we embarked on as a faculty was creating criteria and selection of GAs. In the years past, many of our GAs were selected by chance or due to the fact that we had an opening to fill and they were in our program at the time. At the beginning of our tenure, we posted the list of all the GAs currently in our program. Faculty were surprised that some of our GAs had been in their position for more than five years. Still other GAs weren't working

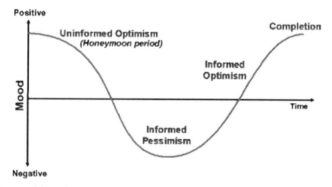

Figure 5.1.   Positive Change Cycle

consistently with any advisor and some were not even actively contributing to the department. Again, faculty were eager to begin to look at the criteria for selection. A committee was quickly formed to investigate.

Two short months later, the optimism had worn thin. As noted earlier, during implementation of any change, uninformed optimism slowly moved on to the informed pessimism stage (Kelly & Conner, 1979). An issue that became a source of debate was what research courses were fundamental to a doctoral program. We had faculty that favored qualitative research courses and others who saw that quantitative methods were of greatest importance. There was an overall dissatisfaction with how research courses were taught. One faculty member went so far as to say, "We can't be held hostage by what we currently offer—we can't wait until something drops from the sky." It is during this dip in implementation that it was important to us to keep our goals in the forefront of our monthly meetings.

SUCCESSES AND OBSTACLES

Facilitating change is always a slow process. Without buy-in from stakeholders changes implemented may be only temporary. We sought to make lasting systemic changes in our graduate programs. As we reflect on the three-year process there were areas where we were able to have a significant impact and areas that are still works in progress. We found the success or failure of an initiative correlated directly with how the initiative was presented as well as how involved faculty and other stakeholders were in decision making. As previously mentioned leadership in higher education can be characterized as either having a *leader*-centric focus or a *community*-centric focus (Dopson et al., 2016). Our focus was to attempt to be *community*-centric in our leadership style as we addressed initiatives we faced in the department. At times this approach was successful and at times there were obstacles we had to face along the way. In this section we attempt to discuss some of these as well as ways we look to move forward in the future.

Conflicting Demands of Leadership

This area was one of the most difficult to navigate. We faced a highly unusual set of circumstances with the leadership transitions taking place in our university, college, and department. Some of these conflicts were merely related to our lack of historical context while others were related to changes in administration and how the decision-making process evolves when there is a high degree of fluidity in personnel who serve in leadership roles.

Conflicting Demands due to Lack of Historical Context

Many conflicting demands we faced were merely a product of our lack of knowledge and contextual understanding of the historical operations of the department and programs. We were both new to our positions and one of us even new to the university. This at times led to conflict merely because we were "someone new" and "someone different." When a new employee enters an organization and attempts to adapt quickly, stakeholders may feel that they are an interloper. This was the case for us quite often during the first two years of our assignment.

On several occasions we would hear statements from our faculty and administration such as "last year we did. . . ." or "in the past we have done . . ." as we tried to implement new protocols and procedures. Finding the best response to these situations was a learning experience. Our strategy became either apply the adage "if it isn't broken don't fix it" or view it as an opportunity to encourage faculty to try a different approach. The best response we found was to listen and honor some of the historical context of what had been done while in some cases applying a more *leader*-centric implementation of a new protocol under the context of "why don't we try this and see how it goes?" Probably one of the most successful strategies we applied in these situations was the establishment of subcommittees to look at various components of programs. Traditionally in many situations there did not seem to be a clear decision-making protocol in place. For example in developing new courses, the process in the past had been a faculty member simply submitting their course to the university approval committee without vetting the course with other faculty. This was completed without consideration of whether there was sufficient student enrollment or if it fit into a prescribed scope and sequence. This led to courses being offered and not having sufficient enrollment, followed by scrambling to find a course for a faculty member to teach to fill their load. One of our biggest successes was using a subcommittee to identify a list of courses and requirements for our PhD program. We then brought the work of this committee to the graduate faculty for a vote of approval. A similar process was used for establishing admissions criterion, and for selecting GAs. This mix of a *leader*-centric pushing the envelope to help facilitate change followed by a *community*-centric democratic process to facilitate consensus proved to be successful in many situations.

Conflicting Demands Related to Administrative Changes

During a three-year period we had a change in chancellor, three changes in provost, and a change in dean. As we looked to restructure many times we were asking questions of individuals who were in interim positions of leadership within the college and university. This added a layer of demand to our positions.

When determining a U.S. News and World Report ranking, the organization surveys education deans, superintendents, and school leaders. For graduate education programs, 40 percent of this ranking is based upon "quality assessment," 42 percent pertains to faculty resources and research productivity, and finally 18 percent addresses "student selectivity". The student selectivity ranking utilizes two variables to determine the university's score. The first is the ratio between the number of students who applied and were accepted and the second, the student's scores on the GRE (Morse & Hines, 2017).

As this initiative trickled down through the administrative ranks to the program level, the focus became looking at initiatives to increase the "student selectivity" score. Therefore, we were given a conflicting directive by being asked to grow programs and increase enrollment while at the same time being more selective in who we admit. For example, in order to increase scores related to "student selectivity" it is favorable to have a higher denial than acceptance ratio in programs. In addition, to increase the score it is desirable to increase the requirements for GRE scores as 6 percent of the ranking is based on the quantitative average score and 6 percent on the verbal average score (Morse & Hines, 2017). Thus, the biggest questions for us became how do we increase enrollment of students overall while requiring them to: (1) have higher GRE scores to be admitted, and (2) deny more of the applications to improve the acceptance rate ratio?

Our solution to this dilemma remains unsolved, but how we addressed this issue did facilitate a successful collaboration within our programs. We utilized data from our previous GRE admissions cycles to identify a soft cut score for the GRE examination. This process also helped us to more clearly define what we were looking for in a doctoral candidate. The process led to the development of an admissions screening committee and rubric to evaluate each candidate's application using five factors, namely academic potential, writing ability, field-related experience and potential, GRE and language acquisition scores, and area of interest match. The establishment of this rubric has led to higher quality candidates. We currently have five students who have doctoral fellowships (competitive awards which provide funding above and beyond the general graduate assistantship at our university). It has also led to more selectivity in our process. We are happy to report that our enrollment has also remained steady for the past three years even with this new process in place.

Balancing the Needs of Faculty with the Needs of Students

One of the most difficult components of facilitating systemic change is trying to balance meeting student needs and improving programs while maintaining balance in faculty workload. Our department currently has forty-seven full-time faculty, some who are clinical, as well as, some that are tenure track. Determining a time to meet face-to-face with this entire group was found to be a nearly impossible task. Since our focus was to facilitate change through *community*-centric versus *leader*-centric means, this became even more difficult to accomplish.

We implemented a strategy that was proven to be effective, which consisted of combining the use of technology via web-based questionnaires and voting paired with monthly face-to-face meetings held at a time frame when the largest percentage of faculty were available. This allowed faculty to provide input on topics of discussion and have a decision-making protocol in place that allowed faculty members to be involved in the process. Our focus was not to overload faculty with multiple meetings, thus increasing time away from their teaching and research agendas, but to have an effective way to obtain input. The establishment of subcommittees for issues again proved to be very effective in managing decision making. For example, a subcommittee was elected from the faculty, that subcommittee developed drafts of the proposal that was under consideration, and then the proposal was sent to faculty for feedback and a vote. This allowed us to be more effective in decision making without cutting into faculty time.

An additional concern our faculty had was ensuring we were effectively meeting student needs without overloading ourselves with advising, and other management duties. Having a doctoral program with over fifty students enrolled and effectively managing those student needs can be overwhelming. Particularly since so many faculty in our department teach in multiple degree programs with few limited to teaching and/or advising in only one specific program. One of the primary strategies we implemented was to have an initial screening of our PhD applicants by programs to identify a faculty member that was willing to work with a student as an advisor. If an advisor could not be identified for the candidate then their application was not reviewed for admission. This step was put in place to ensure we were adequately supporting any student who entered our programs and providing them with the guidance they needed to become successful. It also ensured that faculty were not overloaded with too many advisees to be able to adequately give students the support they need to be successful. This did result in the admission of slightly fewer students into the program but ensured our students were provided the assistance they needed to grow into effective practitioners.

Adapting to the Era of Accountability

As former K–12 practitioners, accountability measures were not new to us. But as higher education practitioners some of the recent requirements for systemic measure of student and program progress were a new challenge. During our second year in our positions we were asked to develop assessment plans for the degree programs which required the identification of data points and assessments that could be reported to show student growth. This led to insightful discussions with faculty and the identification of measures that strengthened our graduate programs overall through the identification of key assessments. It also required us to take a critical look at standards established by accrediting bodies and national organizations to guide in curriculum alignment and assessment. We also participated in an external evaluation of our PhD and EdS programs. Our faculty were involved in every aspect of our assessment visit and we had the positive feedback, and suggestions by the external team led to reframing goals for the future.

LESSONS LEARNED

Facilitating systemic change in higher education requires understanding the academic system while at the same time honoring the community it serves. Through each of our initiatives, we had to balance the needs of our department with the needs of our faculty and students. As stated earlier, when we were not successful with this balance, the initiative faltered. This was definitely the case when we were first working toward establishing criteria for selecting GAs. When we did not seek consensus or asked for feedback, our community quickly reminded us. It is hard to forget the first time we decided to post the names of GAs that we wanted to vote on during a monthly graduate faculty meeting. We did this without thought to showing them the information ahead of time or even coming to a consensus about selection criteria. It was after this misstep that one of the most transformational initiatives was launched: creating a GA selection committee. One faculty member who participated said, "I don't believe in all my time at this university I have ever felt so involved!"

In addition to balancing the needs of the institution with the needs of the individuals, we have learned that good leaders keep focused on the "why" of change. If leaders don't know the "why," then it will be impossible to convince others to work toward end goals. Any time we lost focus of our goals, the progress suffered. We were incredibly fortunate to be in this together. Having another leader to remind you of the "why" is key. Finding others to shoulder the work helps provide the strength needed to make tough decisions. Important lesson learned: you need mentors to continue to support you along the way.

CONCLUSION

Having the chance to reflect on the process of systematic change with all of its obstacles, challenges, and successes has afforded us the opportunity to see the impact of systematic change. Through the process of change, we had to embrace conflict, maintain balance, and support the need for adaptation. In our own experience it was encouraging to know that there were many like-minded faculty who were willing to believe that change in higher education is possible. Change takes time, and we are still writing our story, but as long as we are focused on the "why" and work as a community, change in higher education is possible.

Interviews

"Light bulb moments" are often seen as being serendipitous and fleeting. I hope that the following interview questions and answers deepen understanding about how these moments can be cultivated and sustained. The "Light Bulb Moment Worksheet" (appendix) offers a framework for stimulating transformation at your college or university.

Changing the Light Bulb

David: How many academics does it take to change a light bulb?

Derrick: (Laugher) Wow, that's a fabulous [question]. I think a lot of it depends on the size of the warehouse you're trying to change. I think if you're working with one single department that sometimes it doesn't take quite as many. You have to have a kind of critical mass of people moving the same direction. Systemically though it just gets larger and larger, so I always try to focus on trying to do as much collaboratively with my faculty as I can [so] I can get a sense of "do we have the majority of them turning the light bulb in the same direction or wanting to totally change the entire lighting scheme of a room?"

Jennifer: (Laughter) I guess I would say in academia it is going to be more than one because many people need to give their opinion about the type light bulb you're going to use, the stance that you're going to take. What's the philosophy behind the reason you're changing the light bulb? Is it better to be in darkness than in the light? I mean, you name it. That could actually take a very long time and probably in academia sometimes it just doesn't get changed.

Question for Reader Reflection

To what degree does collaborative culture promote or inhibit transformation initiatives at your college/university?

Change Agency

David: *How has your life prepared you to be a change agent?*

Jennifer: I think that early on, even when I was younger, that I was given opportunities to lead, I was given opportunities to make mistakes. And I think through those [experiences I] built my efficacy.

I think people are given opportunities all the time and just don't take them. And then that means [they] are not strengthening those muscles to make a change. Time and time again . . . I was given leadership positions because no one else wanted it. You know, people want people to lead the charge and to help make change, but there are not a lot of people willing to do that.

It's amazing when someone's given an opportunity and they say "I can't do it." And I look at the person and they have all the tools necessary—they have all of the experience necessary—to be able to make that change and be able to lead that charge. But maybe they're crippled by just feeling . . . an inability or lack of self-confidence.

Derrick: And for me I always felt like the best way to facilitate change and do what was best for students was to constantly be moving forward and exploring new ideas and trying to integrate those into your curriculum and your programs. And so I think for me I've never really considered myself a change agent, but I always wanted to do what was best for students. And what was best for students was staying on the cutting edge of what was happening. And that led to just various things that [I] ended up getting involved with.

Question for Reader Reflection

What motivates you to reach your potential as a change agent? What inhibits you from realizing your potential as a change agent?

Advice

David: *What advice do you have for others who want to transform higher education?*

Derrick: Well I think one thing Jennifer and I did very quickly, that was actually a whim when we did it, [was to start] our meetings with this very simple thing that I had learned several years ago. We just called it a Cudos Session [in] that we started meetings with "let's talk about either something that's happened professionally or personally." We did a five minute opening . . . and of course faculty say "hey, I got accepted to this conference" or "I got this manuscript accepted here to this particular journal" or faculty would say, "hey, my daughter is pregnant, I'm going to have a grandchild" or you know those type of things. We created that forum and it was something we did just as a [way of] trying to make something that is so clinical, in a meeting format, into a more open discussion and were always amazed with how that began to change the culture. And so one of the biggest pieces of advice if somebody that's new, that's coming into this kind of role, is never forget that everybody is a person and they've all got things going on—on campus and off campus—and create a time to connect with people personally, not just professionally. I think that's a big thing that I felt has led to being able to move some things forward because I realize different people have different things on their plate and they're able to do things, or not able to do things, based on the situation they're in.

Jennifer: I would say get people [at work] and in your life that will really inform you. Find people that disagree with you, find people that agree with you, but . . . have people that are informing you that maybe don't believe that same as you [do]. And also people that can support you and give you that confidence that you need. You need . . . mentors, people at your university that you can rely on—you can close the door and say "what should I do?"—that are going to be straight shooters with you. And even somebody outside of that. I would say I've relied on people that are outside of my department, that may be even in a different college, that have a different perspective.

Question for Reader Reflection

How could a Cudos Session and/or critical friends be cultivated at your college or university to help facilitate transformation?

REFERENCES

Dopson, S., Ferlie, E., McGivern, G., Fischer, M. D., Ledger, J., Behrens, S., & Wilson, S. (2016). *The impact of leadership and leadership development in higher education: A review of the literature and evidence.* London: Leadership Foundation for Higher Education. (Research and development series).

Fullan, M. (2007). *The new meaning of educational change* (4th ed.). New York, NY: Teachers College Press.

Hord, S. M., & Roussin, J. L. (2013). *Implementing change through learning: Concerns-based concepts, tools, and strategies for guiding change.* Thousand Oaks, CA: Corwin Press.

Kelly, D., & Conner, D. R. (1979). The emotional cycle of change. In J. E. Jones & J. W. Pfeiffer (Eds.), *The 1979 annual handbook for group facilitators* (pp. 117–121). La Jolla, CA: University Associates.

Morse, R., & Hines, K. (March 13, 2017). *Methodology: 2018 best education schools rankings—Find out how U.S. News ranks graduate education programs.* Retrieved from https://www.usnews.com/education/best-graduate-schools/articles/education-schools-methodology

Conclusion

So how many academics will it take to change the light bulb at your college or university?

0?
1 or 2?
3 or More?
Top-Down and Bottom-Up Contributors?
An Elastic Number Based on the Scope of Work?

Ultimately, the value of the case studies and interviews offered in this teaching and learning text will be determined by how helpful they are to you and to your team as you pursue meaningful change at your institution.

Here are some of the high-impact lessons learned by chapter authors from Roosevelt University (IL), SUNY, The College at Brockport (NY), American College of Education (IN), University of Pittsburgh (PA), and University of Arkansas (AR):

- Stay focused on the "why" of change
- Relationships matter
- Honest feedback is a gift
- Creating change is sometimes easier than maintaining change
- Raise awareness about Organizational Change Theory
- Listen to input from a wide variety of constituents
- Begin meetings with a "Cudos Session"
- Seek mentors who are willing to disagree with you
- Work collaboratively to sustain momentum and prevent burnout
- Develop a cohort that transcends role and rank

My interviews with chapter authors suggest that there is also great value in accounting for what—in your own life—has led you to being an agent of change. Identifying your own resilience, flexibility, and motivation is a key lever for change and can be a powerful vehicle for self-realization, self-expression, and institutional contribution.

Last is the surprising revelation that many authors shared about the inherent value of reflecting on the initiatives described in their respective chapters. Honestly, this outcome was a surprise to me as well. I hope that it provides a rationale for academics across the country to invest the time and energy needed for a well-deserved period of authentic reflection for personal fulfillment and professional growth.

Appendix

Light Bulb Moment Worksheet

Usually when we talk about someone having a "light bulb moment" we are referring to a surprise occurrence that enlightens thought and action. During the process of compiling the case studies and interviews for this book I came to wonder if "light bulb moments" can be cultivated—both as individuals and as institutions. To that end, I invite you to use this worksheet to cultivate intentional change at your institution and within yourself.

1. Identify what you want to change: _____

_____

2. Reflect on how your life experience fuels your investment in this issue and informs your vision for successful outcomes.
3. Consider advice from case studies and interviews and write down four lessons that could help you generate meaningful change.

Lesson #1   Lesson #2

Lesson #3   Lesson #4

4. Identify mid-range dates on your calendar (e.g., one month, end of semester, end of school year) to reflect on your progress and do yourself the favor of pausing long enough to reflect at those times.
5. Celebrate victories and modify strategies as needed.

About the Editor

David Silverberg, EdD, is the director of the Telego Center for Educational Improvement at Ashland University in Ohio, where he produces professional development workshops, research and evaluation projects, and customized training events. Silverberg received his doctoral and master's degrees in education from Pepperdine University, California, and his bachelor's degree from Wesleyan University, Connecticut. His nearly thirty years in the field of education include experience as a professor, researcher, administrator, and teacher.

About the Contributors

Imani Akin, PhD, is academic curriculum director, American College of Education, Indiana.

Jennifer G. Beasley, EdD, is director of Teacher Education, Boyer Center for Student Service, University of Arkansas.

Brad Cawn, AbD, is adjunct professor of language and literature, Roosevelt University, Illinois.

Heather Donnelly is visiting assistant professor, SUNY, The College at Brockport, New York.

Sarah Grubb is visiting laboratory instructor, University of Pittsburgh, Pennsylvania.

Nancy Kaufmann, PhD, is assistant director of Undergraduate Research, University of Pittsburgh, Pennsylvania.

Jeff Linn, PhD, is department chair, SUNY, The College at Brockport, New York.

Derrick Mears, PhD, is clinical associate professor and EdS program coordinator, Department of Curriculum and Instruction, CIED, University of Arkansas.

Crystal Neumann, DBA, is chair of the Leadership Department, American College of Education, Indiana.

Marcie Warner is laboratory instructor, Department of Biological Sciences, University of Pittsburgh, Pennsylvania.